I0134543

A Hero's Journey

Erik J. Ekstrom

And Friends

A Hero's Journey

©Copyright 2014 Erik J. Ekstrom and Friends
Compiled by Vigilante Publishing Group LLC.
Contributions Copyright© 2008-2014

All rights reserved. This book or any portion thereof may not be reproduced or used in any manner whatsoever without the express written permission of the publisher except for the use of brief quotations in a book review.

Vigilante Publishing Group LLC.
PO Box 668
Scottsdale, AZ. 85252-0668

This book can be purchased through major book retailers in all countries.

Printed in the United States of America.

First Printing

01052014

ISBN: 0692027025
ISBN: 9780692027028

Contributors

Jaclyn Boser
Rev. Andrea Boyungs
Kevin A. Cain
Tyler Lee Caverly
Cathy Droz
Erik J. Ekstrom
Pamala Kim Everts
Kate Watkins Furman
Jeremiah Gager
Jennifer Oneal Gunn
Saundra R. Hays
Dixon Hill
Matt Imbordino
Abby Krause
Ivy Kingsland
Laura Levendofske
Barbara Lindley
Irene Lowe
H.E.M.
Gina M. Makowsky
Anthony Marceau
Calvin Marcus
Jeffery Pearson
Irena Rojo-Horodynska
Sheree L. Rondo
X.S.
Joseph Scheidel
P.J. Scheidel
Virginia Thom
Jason Webb
Percy Webb
Roger Wyer

Reviews

"A special thank you to Mr. Ekstrom and to all of the lovely people who contributed to this lovely book. As my husband has been stationed in Afghanistan for the last eight months, my two young children and I are always fighting the sadness of his absence, but now we read through A Hero's Journey every night before bedtime and it makes the days easier for all of us. Bless you all."

"I found this book and gave it to my family before leaving for my tour. I think it helped them get through the rough times and I appreciate the heart felt words inscribed within. I salute you all for this."

"My daddy has been away for a very long time. My mommy helped me get pictures of my daddy and we pasted them inside the book which is next to my bed. We read through it every night."

"I have found it difficult with my wife being away. I am so proud of her. She is serving the military in such a capacity that I do worry every day. I have used the journal pages with my son to keep her safe and sound in our hearts. We thank you for such a wonderfully compiled book. As I am a spiritual man, I find the Lord has worked through you all and has brought peace to our family. Thank you for this sense of peace and good will. I also noticed that all of the profits of this book will be donated and I commend you for your spiritual charity."

Forward

There are many ways to thank our troops for their service to this great nation and this is my personal contribution. A Hero's Journey is a book of memories, dedicated to our troops at home and abroad, and the families who remain strong in their absence. A Hero's Journey is an uplifting anthology of poetry, short stories, letters, music and so much more, with over thirty contributors from across this beautiful country.

I had an idea a few years back, one that would inspire men, women and children across the country to join up and contribute to A Hero's Journey Project. After seeing the desperation of the families of our men and women in uniform serving in a foreign land, and the sadness of not knowing if or when they would return home, I decided to put the notion of A Hero's Journey Project out to the masses via social media and by word of mouth. The response I received was absolutely incredible and soon the stories, poems and so forth began coming to my email from across the country. Both young and old discussed their loved ones who fought for our country and their pride was illuminated through their words. Everyone wanted to get involved and so the journey began.

My intentions are that this beautifully crafted anthology, A Hero's Journey, will bring hope to those who have lost it, and create an outlet for their pain with its journal and photograph pages located within this book. I encourage you to write down your thoughts of your loved ones serving this great nation and put special photographs of them within the dedicated pages. It is my belief that A Hero's Journey can help those who have buried their feelings deep inside. I truly believe it is time to open up and let your feelings flow.

A Hero's Journey is a keepsake for veterans and anyone who is either in the military, has a family member serving or knows of someone who does. I put this book out with the utmost respect for all and salute you for all you have done throughout the years to protect our nation from threats both foreign and domestic.

Erik J. Ekstrom

Editor's Note

Dear Readers,

I hope you greatly enjoy the efforts of the author and his friends who contributed their work. It took guts to sit down and write how they felt about their loved ones openly. To the soldiers, we want you to know how much we appreciate you all and what you do. This compilation piece depicts all eras of war and all sides of it, from the families that miss their loved one, to the loved one being away, to the fallen. Please read, enjoy, and think of the moment when you will be with your beloved and brave soldier once again.

For all the brave men and women of the military who courageously protect our country and the families who patiently await their safe return.

All proceeds of A Hero's Journey will go to the Gary Sinise Foundation.

At the Gary Sinise Foundation, we serve our Nation by honoring our defenders, veterans, first responders, their families, and those in need.

http://www.garysinisefoundation.org/

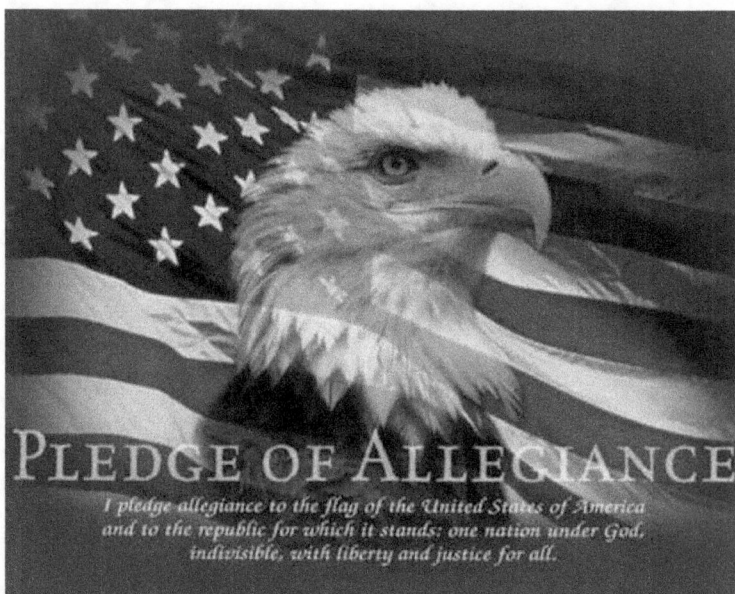

PLEDGE OF ALLEGIANCE

I pledge allegiance to the flag of the United States of America and to the republic for which it stands: one nation under God, indivisible, with liberty and justice for all.

The Journey

A man, a time
His youth, his prime
A call, a sign
His life on the line

He feels the fright
He pushes on with might
His home is in sight
He'll never give up
His undaunting fight

His kids, his wife
An unfinished life
It cuts like a knife
The pain and the strife

The end is near
I'm coming home, my dear
There is no fear
Please, oh please
Don't shed a tear

Erik J. Ekstrom

The Song of the Warrior

Since Daddy's gone away to war
When night comes, dark and deep,
My mama sings a special song
To help me go to sleep.

It is a song of warriors
All marching to the fight,
While singing our great battle hymn
'Till morning brings the light.

"Sleep now my precious little child
Sleep now in love and peace,
You daddy will be coming home
The guns of war will cease."

It is a sweet and wondrous song
Sung by the brave and free,
Ringing out through fruitful fields
From sea to shining sea

Kate Watkins Furman

Sacrifice

As I look at the pictures of my unborn son,
I can't help but feel guilty that I'll miss his birth.
We have two other children, this is our last one.
I love them all equally, for everything they're worth.

I'm in the military and have always been prepared
For the chance to serve my country and do my job.
I've never left my family, so we're a little scared.
As we say our good-byes, we try hard not to sob.

I grab my bags and gear, board the plane, and fly away.
It's a very long flight, which gives me time to ponder.
As I sit here and think of all the things I wanted to say,
I remember, "Absence makes the heart grow fonder."

Nobody likes the idea of going off to fight in a war,
But that's the nature of the world in times like this.
There's always going to be a good cause to fight for,
Like banning together against the bad people that exist.

We battle all day against an enemy that's got nothing to lose,
Who shoot at us with anger, not caring who they kill.
We fight for everything that's good because we choose
To help rid the world of evil men and their murderous will.

I've missed my family and thought of them every day.
I've carried their pictures with me no matter where I'd go.
As I lie here dying, I pray for my wife who's so far away.
I think of my unborn son and a father he'll never know.

It's been years since I passed away and I miss my wife.
From above, I've watched my son grow into a find young man.
He placed a plaque at my grave that was the motto of my life.
This is what he wrote, may it help others to understand:

"A soldier's duty is to protect the innocent and their rights.
Lady Liberty is our backbone and strength, we fight for her.
Whether you agree or disagree with the wars we fight,
If you can use your freedom to protest, thank a soldier."

P.J. Scheidel

The Orange Dragon Stops

"Hi, Jennifer!"

"Hi."

"Are you riding the bus today?"

"No."

"Oh, then you're waiting for a ride?"

"Yes."

"From who?"

"From my mom and dad."

"Oh…b-but they're in Iraq aren't they?"

"Billy, d'you know how many seats are on our buses?"

"Uh, 'bout thirty-three?"

"No, *more!*"

"Why?"

"'Cause."

"'Cause *why?*"

"'Cause, not even seventeen of our big buses filled up are enough to drive to that horrible place where our moms and dads and brothers are living…"

H.E.M.

Waking

Those nights you read to me
Of sinking pirate ships,
Violet moonlight on shark filled water,
I loved to look up at you,
Touch your rough cheek,
With the smooth skin of my small hand,
As I drifted into sleep's warm waters.

Listening to you voice,
First low and scary, then loud and brave,
Shouting lines over clean white decks,
Echoes certain to bring a mother,
A wrinkle of feigned displeasure on her face.

Carried away too soon by those strange ships,
Only sleep separated us then,
And maybe it still does,
But waking is harder,
Even night's silent waves no friend,
Since the story ended
And only one of us came back.

Laura Levendofske

Together Again

Ripped apart is how you feel
Nothing in this world seems real
You're here on Earth, but feel incomplete
But this is something you can beat

There's pieces of you everywhere
To smile or laugh has become so rare
But, keep your chin up, on that it depends
If your pieces will be brought together again

It's heartbreaking and lonely, every day is full of tears
You thought this would never happen, if you lived a million years
But life's full of surprises, full of things we can't control
All we can do is try our best to make sure we stay whole

Of course, we fall apart sometimes, when life becomes demanding
But we're always taken care of, loved ones are so understanding
There are people who take care of us, people we know are always
there
Even with the best of friends, sometimes life isn't fair

Pull yourself together with the help of those you love
It's okay if it takes time, it's important not to shove
Soon you'll see that even though you've lost your true best friend
There's hope in believing that someday you'll be together again

Jaclyn Boser

Lessons

When I was a child,
Life was quite simple.
All hurts were made better,
With a smile and a dimple.

"Mom, he's bothering me!"
Rang through the house.
My brother would run and hide.
Quiet as a mouse.

Dad came home,
Super was made.
Eat, talk, and share,
Together at home we stayed.

Now I am grown,
With family still close.
I have children of my own,
To love and cherish.

The lessons of love,
Are close to my heart.
To my family,
I will impart.

Rev. Andrea Boyungs

Alone

Rattling around
Inside yourself
You think
You're alone

Looking around
At blank faces
You think
You're alone

Listening around
To silly talk
You think
You're alone

You've lost your connection
To everyone
To yourself
To God

Roger Wyer (Author of *Choosing Joy at Work*)

Over and Out of Seas and Time

You are the breeze
The trees
You are my dreams
My sleep
Don't worry or weep
Overseas
You still oversee us
There's no in between

Calvin Markus

Bittersweet

It's not often that we speak
Days pass by, sometimes weeks
You're helping out our country
So why does it feel so bittersweet?
I pray to God that you'll come home
I'm still not used to feeling so alone
I keep your picture in my pocket
And sometimes wear your cologne
I smile with you, I laugh
It's no secret, you're my other half
Miles apart, my smiles faded
I wish you weren't in the draft
I count the days 'til you leave Iraq
We'll kiss so much, you'll forget to unpack
Until that day, remember this
I miss you, I love you, I want you back

We are not lost until found

Abby Krause

Our Heroes

Name:
Relation:
Date of Birth:
Age:
Military Branch:
Rank:
Location/Stationed:
Date:

Our Heroes

Name:
Relation:
Date of Birth:
Age:
Military Branch:
Rank:
Location/Stationed:
Date:

Autumn Lullaby

The sun has gone from the shining skies,
Bye, baby, bye,
The Dandelions have closed their eyes,
Bye, baby, bye.
The stars are lighting their lamps to see
If babies and squirrels and birds and bees
Are sound asleep as they should be,
Bye, baby, bye.

The squirrel keeps warm in his furs of gray,
Bye, baby, bye,
'Neath feathers, birdies are tucked away,
Bye, baby, bye.
In yellow jackets, the bees sleep tight
And cuddle close through the chilly night,
My baby's snug in her gown of white,
Bye, baby, bye.

The squirrel nests in a big oak tree,
Bye, baby, bye.
He finds a hole in the trunk you see,
Bye, baby, bye.
The robin's home is a nest o'erhead
The bees, they nest in a hive instead,
My baby's nest is her little bed,
Bye, baby, bye.

Traditional

Slumber Time is Drawing Near

Slumber time is drawing near
Night is gath'ring round us.
Stars will be bright and clear
When the sandman has found us
Dream sweet dreams the long night through
Mother will be near you
Go to sleep my dear one

Traditional Swedish

Thousands of candles can be lighted
From a single candle,
And the life of the candle will not be shortened,
Happiness never decreases by being shared.

Buddha

A Prayer for the Way to Peace

Father of love, hear my prayer
Help me to know your will
And to do it with courage and faith
Accept my offering of myself
All my thoughts, words, deeds, and sufferings
May my life be spent giving you glory
Give me the strength to follow your call
So that your truth may live in my heart
And bring peace to me and to those I meet
For I believe in your love

Prayer for Courage in the Time of Battle

O, prince of peace, we ask your humble protection
For all our men and women in military service
Give them unflinching courage to defend
With honor, dignity, and devotion
The rights of all who are imperiled
By injustice and evil
By their rock, their shield, and their stronghold
And let them draw their strength from you
For you are God, for ever and ever.

United States Conference of Catholic Bishops

★ ★ ★

_____

_____

_____

_____

_____

_____

_____

_____

_____

_____

_____

_____

_____

_____

_____

_____

_____

_____

_____

_____

_____

_____

_____

_____

★ ★ ★

_____
_____
_____
_____
_____
_____
_____
_____
_____
_____
_____
_____
_____
_____
_____
_____
_____
_____
_____
_____
_____
_____

★ ★ ★

_____

_____

_____

_____

_____

_____

_____

_____

_____

_____

_____

_____

_____

_____

_____

_____

_____

_____

_____

_____

_____

_____

_____

_____

★ ★ ★

_____
_____
_____
_____
_____
_____
_____
_____
_____
_____
_____
_____
_____
_____
_____
_____
_____
_____
_____
_____
_____
_____
_____
_____

★ ★ ★

This Nation will remain the land of the free only so long as it is the home of the brave.
~Elmer Davis

'Geronimo-E KIA'
May 1st, 2011

Untitled #1

I see the heat of my breath dissipate
As do other's lives
I see them sit and think
I see them cry
Lives free from the pain
Eyes free once again
As I look I cannot see
The pain inside
It's too intense to describe
Too intense to prescribe
I see them suffer
I see them flee
I can only dream
For them to be free
As we are
Not as they are

Tyler Lee Caverly

The First of June

I saw a child on top of a dune.
Seemed so long ago, felt like the first of June
I know that day for it was your birth
My ode to my country became my curse
I knew then what I must do
I must be bold and strong for you
Your face envisioned in in my mind
Such innocence and love so divine
Your smile is what I remember most
The feeling of your breath when tucked asleep so close
You have the bluest eyes just like me
Passed generation to generation through the family tree
You are my child! My joy! My light!
This is why I must do what feels right
To know that I will come back to you again
To stare into the face of my best of friends
I saw a child on top of a dune
I remember now…it was the first of June

Jeffrey Pearson

Images So Clear

Images so clear
Thoughts never forgotten
So far and yet so near
His name is Morgottyn

Images so clear
His face is in my mind
Missing him so dear
His state I wish to find

Images so clear
Rushing round my head
War it is a fear
Worrying he may be dead

Images so clear
Why must he be away?
Left with all his gear
Not much that I could say

Images so clear
His call to war had come
I had to shed a tear
Will there ever be a sun

Images so clear
My dear, sweet, Morgottyn
My prayers I wish you'd hear
You shall never be forgotten

Ivy Kingsland

Little Ones

You might not understand this now
Right in this present tense
But as you get older it will slowly start to make sense
Your parent went away to fight in a war
And was never to return
That only has you confused
And for that parent you must naturally yearn
What can be held in your heart is something to be proud of so
much
And that is the fact that your parent was there to protect all of us
So keep them alive with smiling memories and such
And know that as proud of them as you are
They will always love you that much

Kevin A. Cain

Remembering the Day America Was Attacked

"Hi, Billy, wanna play?"

"Sure I got this neato game on my new Playstation 3!"

"Cool, what's it called?"

"Jennifer Goes to War."

"Hey, that's my name!"

"Yeah, I know, don't be silly! Of course, that's you."

"No it's not! I'm not silly!"

"Okay, well, ya wanna just play soldier? You can be the special forces marine."

"Um, I don't like this game anymore, let's play something else."

"Um, okay. What?"

"I dunno, I just want to go home…"

H.E.M.

Six Months

For six months I head to work, a ship tied to a pier
I just returned from the Persian Gulf
To you, my little girl, the one I hold most dear

From morning 'til night, I chip and paint
The salty ocean covered my ship with rust
But happily, I come home to you, my princess, every day

The painting is done, now everything looks new
The next six months I watch the planes land on my ship
This time, it's fourteen days before I see you

The small planes are orange and white
They fly all day as I sail along the Florida coast
I call to hear your precious laugh and wish you good night

The next six months, I have to come and go
My ship is faster and ready to fight
I am surprised to see how much you've grown

The next six months I will be in oceans across the world
You send me letters, cards, and all of your love
My hero is you, my brave little girl

Irene Lowe

Little Soldier Boy

Daddy said he will be back
Mommy said the same
I just wonder if this world
Is playing some game

I am only a little guy
Living with my mother
I have toys, books, TV
I don't have a father

When I'm back from my school
Standing at the door
Mommy says that one day
There will be no more war

That's the time
When my dad
Will come play with me
I'm afraid
By this time
I may be too big

I'm afraid of many things
But I know in my heart
That my dad
For this day
Must be far apart

Missing you,
I asked mom
Playing with my toys
To write this down
And sign it,
Little Soldier Boy

Irena Rojo-Horodynska

Never Alone

Sometimes it seems like no one's there
And everything has changed
Things aren't what they used to be
You can't help feeling strange

All the things you used to do
Like stories before bed
Or Christmas trees or trick or treat
The things your parents did

It all seems so far away now
Like it's never coming back
You still treasure the memories
But new ones are what you lack

But you mustn't forget good times
Keep your happy past alive
Hold onto great times you had
For this you have to strive

For if you don't forget them
They'll really never leave
You'll keep them with you, in your heart
If you just believe

So when it seems you're by yourself
Think of all that you've shared
Carry it with you and remember
You're never alone, don't be scared

Jaclyn Boser

Reflections

My son is a soldier, on his way to Iraq
God, I'd give my life to have him back
Back on the ball field playing with friends
Or on a camp out with his cub scout den
Back in his room with all of his toys
Or building a tree house with the neighborhood boys
Back in the tux he rented for Prom
Or out in the yard chasing his dog
Back in the garage playing drums with his band
Or out by the pool looking so tanned
But my little boy is now a grown man
And no longer needs me to hold onto his hand
The night he called to tell us good bye
I was so torn between fear and pride
So proud of my son yet afraid he would die
I'll remember his words for the rest of my life
"Mom, please don't cry, I'll be just fine
There's no need to worry, you can let your fears rest
I'm a US Marine and we're the best."

Barbara Lindley

Lost Time

I went away
Seems as though
Just the other day
Yet time has passed
It went so fast
It'll be eighteen months this May

My wife
Distraught
My kids
Lost in thought
When will I get home?
From the war I fought

I'm sorry to say
It's not next week
Or even yesterday
I'm coming home
In another month
For just two weeks
To rest my weary bones

I have to say
I'm lost in time
Forever is a minute
It's such a crime
To be away
From the ones I love
So sad for us all
But I'll see you soon

Erik J. Ekstrom

Our Heroes

Name:
Relation:
Date of Birth:
Age:
Military Branch:
Rank:
Location/Stationed:
Date:

Our Heroes

Name:
Relation:
Date of Birth:
Age:
Military Branch:
Rank:
Location/Stationed:
Date:

Hush, My Baby
Don't You Cry

Hush, my baby, don't you cry,
Daddy's gonna come home by and by.
He will bring to his dear little baby
Candy and a kitty and a puppy dog maybe.
Hush, hush, hush and don't you cry,
Daddy's gonna come home by and by.

Traditional

Let Peace Begin With Me

Let there be peace on earth,
And let it begin with me.
Let there be peace on earth,
The peace that was meant to be.
With God as our Father,
Brothers all are we,
Let me walk with my brother,
In perfect harmony.
Let peace begin with me,
Let this be the moment now,
With every step I take,
Let this be my solemn vow,
To take each moment and live each moment
In peace, eternally.
Let there be peace on earth,
And let it begin with me.

Lyrics and Music by Jill Jackson and Sy Miller

He who serves me most,
Who serves his country best.

Homer

Buddhist Payer for Peace

May all beings everywhere plagued
With sufferings of the body and mind
Quickly be freed from their illnesses.
May those frightened cease to be afraid,
And may those bound be free.
May the powerless find power,
And may people think of befriending on another.
May those who find themselves in trackless, fearful wilderness—
The children, the age, the unprotected—
Be guarded by beneficial celestials,
And may they swiftly attain Buddhahood.

Angels Watching Over Me

All night, all day,
Angels watching over me, my Lord
All night, all day,
Angels watching over me

Sun is a-setting in the west,
Angels are watching over me, my Lord
Sleep my child, take your rest,
Angels watching over me

All night, all day,
Angels watching over me, my Lord
All night, all day,
Angels watch over me

When at night I go to sleep
Angels watching over me, my Lord
Pray the lord my soul to keep
Angels watching over me

American Spiritual

★ ★ ★

_____
_____
_____
_____
_____
_____
_____
_____
_____
_____
_____
_____
_____
_____
_____
_____
_____
_____
_____
_____
_____
_____

★ ★ ★

_____

_____

_____

_____

_____

_____

_____

_____

_____

_____

_____

_____

_____

_____

_____

_____

_____

_____

_____

_____

_____

_____

_____

My Dove

You make me laugh when I want to cry
You're honest to me, you have never lied
When my fears disappear
You make my problems seem so clear
The lord created you from the stars above
He sent you from heaven for me to love
I'll give the angels back their wings
Their golden harps and all their things
I never thought I'd feel this way
I figured now I need to pray
While I'm here and you are there
I'll send you my soul as I kneel in prayer
Thank you Lord for the path you've paved
Give me strength in this hour
Give to me the highest power
Send a message to the one I love
Tell him I am sending my turtle dove
One that is white and has my spirits within
Tell him if he cries that it's not a sin
Lord watch over him as he is overseas
And then dear Lord bring my daddy back to me

Sheree L. Rondo

I am Old Glory

I am Old Glory: For more than ten score years I have been the banner of hope and freedom for generation after generation of Americans.

Born amid the first flames of America's fight for freedom, I am the symbol of a country that has grown from a little group of thirteen colonies to a united nation of fifty sovereign states.

Planted firmly on the high pinnacle of American faith my gently fluttering folds have proved an inspiration to untold millions.

Men have followed me into battle with unwavering courage.

They have looked upon me as a symbol of national unity.

They have prayed that they and their fellow citizens might continue to enjoy the life, liberty, and pursuit of happiness, which has been granted to every American as the heritage of free men.

So long as men love liberty more than life itself, so long as they treasure the priceless privileges bought with the blood of our forefathers, so long as the principles of truth, justice, and charity for all remain deeply rooted in human hearts, I shall continue to be the enduring banner of the United States of America.

Master Sergeant Percy Webb, USMC.

Time

The pain I feel
When I'm away
I miss you, dear
I wish I had stayed

I'm coming back
For just two weeks
On a little R and R
So please don't weep

I'm headed back
For another tour
Back home in fifteen months
And not a day sooner

So don't forget me
And never let me go
You're in my heart
This I pray you know

Erik J. Ekstrom

Understanding Sacrifice

"A soldier's duty is to protect the innocent and their rights.
Lady Liberty is our backbone and strength, we fight for her.
Whether you agree or disagree with the wars we fight,
If you can use your freedom to protest, thank a soldier."

I read the plaque one more time before leaving,
Hoping for a sign to show me that my dad is here.
I've always thought that seeing was believing,
But, in my heart, my dad will always be near.

I have no real memories of my dad.
He died months before I was even born.
I'm proud of who he was, but I'm still very sad.
Most days, the feelings in my heart are really torn.

It's pretty hard growing up without a father,
Not having that male role model there when you need him.
Some days I'd cry, and wouldn't want to be bothered.
The light at the end of the tunnel seemed kind of dim.

Things were rough, but I had the love of my mother.
She taught me what it means to really sacrifice.
Some years were much harder to get through than others,
But we stuck together, made a choice, and rolled the dice.

My father, along with all the men in his unit,
Made a promise to each other the day they deployed.
If any one of them should somehow not make it,
The rest would help watch over their little girls and boys.

They also vowed to watch over any widowed wife
And be there for her as an extended family.
Most of those men were a huge influence in my life.
I am forever grateful that they were there for me.

The bond that those men have is something to treasure.
They lay their lives on the line for a cause worth fighting.
The freedoms they give are impossible to measure.
That's why, now that I'm eighteen, I'm enlisting.

P.J. Scheidel

As Above So Below

If truth means we be golden fish freed,
Waves of synchronized intent,
Purpose made transparent.
Will certainty allow for freedom?

Aware servitude, such a pleasant fall,
To embrace pure instinct,
Does matter resonate
If the tune written is but enjoyed?

Can just knowledge employed,
Give choice to simpler label, peace?
Or does the naming but diminish?

Laura Levendofske

A Prayer

Sometimes at night
When I look upon the stars
I think about your majesty
And always like
In the real dream
You walk along the stars with me
And in my eyes
You can see my doubt
But I know only you
You are the one
Who can wake me up
And show the way and show the truth
Sometimes at night
When I take a little break
I think about your greatest love
And always like
In real life
I feel I never get enough
And in my heart
You can see a space
But I know in my soul
There is a voice
That tells me
I'm not missing anything at all

Irena Rojo-Horodynska

Alone They Weep

Red and white, blue and stars
'Neath these colors do we sleep
In peace and comfort while they fight
Wives and mothers, alone, they weep

They fight for us, masters of their fear
Keeping the foe back, always back
Letter to home are all they get
Before they press the next attack

No mistakes can they make
The penalty, death, its cold dark hand
Grasping and pulling souls to death's door
Of their lives, they have no more command

Some can be helped, brought back from Hell
Saved by the hands of a red cross on white
Pain for a lifetime, but better than death
The price paid by some, so others can still fight

Some lay there bleeding, some calm others frantic
In the arms of a comrade, they look to the sky
Some can't cheat death, they wait for the light
To take them away, quietly they die

The battle still rages, others will fall
The price for our beloved freedom is death
Politicians fight for freedom, that's what they say
Sitting in comfort, wasting their breath

Red and white, blue and stars
'Neath these colors do our soldiers sleep
Sent home to families, never to wake
Wives and mothers, alone, they weep

Jason Webb

My Legacy

Brass and gold
Olive and rose
Jade and sapphire
So very different
Yet so much the same

Their smiles dim the heavens
Their beauty surpasses that of Aphrodite
Hearts more pure than the first snow
With spirits as strong as a wild stallion
Laughter so light and melodic like music from a flute

Their eyes possess the mischief of the fairies
And the wisdom of the ages
They love without question
Hope without fear
Then even kiss away my tears

They are my gift to this world
They are my life
My heart
My very soul
These girls are my legacy

Rev. Andrea Boyungs

Crazy Times

Who brought you into this mess?
Who picked this place for you?
Who said this is your time?
Who dealt these cards?

Who, who, who?

Who played this dirty trick?
Who thought this would be fun?
Who delivered you here?
In these crazy times?

You, you, you!

You love excitement
You are tougher than tough
You are a player
You got game

You came with something
You alone can give
You have to make a difference
As only you can

You chose the time
You chose the place
You love it wide open
You chose these crazy times

Roger Wyer, Author of *Choosing Joy at Work*

Take Me As I Am

I've come back
Yet I'm not the same
It'll take me a while
Be patient

I am hesitant
To see you now
For I have changed
Be patient

I am still your mom
But war has changed me
I still love you
Be patient

There are stories to share
And even more I won't
Don't be afraid
Be patient

I will still hold you
Maybe tighter than before
Yet I may back away
Be patient

You are my love
My whole world
Please be patient
And take me as I am

Erik J. Ekstrom

Our Heroes

Name:
Relation:
Date of Birth:
Age:
Military Branch:
Rank:
Location/Stationed:
Date:

Our Heroes

Name:
Relation:
Date of Birth:
Age:
Military Branch:
Rank:
Location/Stationed:
Date:

Star Spangled Banner

O! Say can you see by the dawn's early light,
What so proudly we hailed at the twilight's last gleaming,
Whose broad stripes and bright stars through the perilous fight,
O'er the ramparts we watched, were so gallantly streaming?
And the rocket's red glare, the bombs bursting in air,
Gave proof through the night that our flag was still there.

O! Say does that star-spangled banner yet wave,
O'er the land of the free and the home of the brave?

On the shore dimly seen through the mists of the deep,
Where the foe's haughty host in dread silence reposes,
What is that which the breeze, o'er the towering steep,
As it fitfully blows, half conceals, half discloses?
Now it catches the gleam of the morning's first beam,
In full glory reflected now shines in the stream.

Tis the star-spangled banner, O! Long may it wave,
O'er the land of the free and the home of the brave.

And where is that band who so vauntingly swore
That the havoc of war and the battle's confusion,
A home and a country, shall leave us no more?
Their blood has washed out their foul footsteps pollution.
No refuge could save the hireling and slave,
From the terror of fight or the gloom of the grave.

And the star-spangled banner in triumph doth wave,
O'er the land of the free and the home of the brave.

O! Thus be it ever when freemen shall stand,
Between their loved home and the war's desolation,
Blest with victory and peace, may the heav'n rescued land,
Praise the power that hath made and preserved us a nation!
Then conquer we must, when our cause it is just,
And this be our motto- "In God Is Our Trust,"
And the star-spangled banner in triumph shall wave,
O'er the land of the free and the home of the brave.

Francis Scott Key

God Bless the U.S.A.

If tomorrow all the things were gone
I'd worked for all my life,
And I had to start again
With just my children and my wife,
I'd thank my lucky stars
To be living here today,
'Cause the flag still stands for freedom
And they can't take that away.

I'm proud to be an American
Where at least I know I'm free,
And I won't forget the men who died
Who gave that right to me,
And I gladly stand up next to you
And defend her still today,
'Cause there ain't no doubt I love this land
God bless the U.S.A

From the lakes of Minnesota
To the hills of Tennessee,
Across the plains of Texas
From sea to shining sea.
From Detroit down to Houston
And New York to L.A.,
There's pride in every American heart
And it's time we stand and say:

I'm proud to be an American
Where at least I know I'm free,
And I won't forget the men who died
Who gave that right to me,
And I gladly stand up next to you
And defend her still today,
'Cause there ain't no doubt I love this land
God bless the U.S.A.

Lee Greenwood

The price of greatness is responsibility.

Winston Churchill

Prayer for Families and Friends Left at Home

O God, protector of all people and nations,
Protect my family and friends at home
From the violence and evil of others.
Keep them safe from the weapons of hate and destruction
And guard them against the deeds of evildoers.
Grant them your protection and care
In tranquility and peace.
Grant this through Christ our Lord.

United States Conference of Catholic Bishops

Prayer for the Safety of Soldiers

Almighty and eternal God,
Those who take refuge in you will be glad
And forever will shout for joy.
Protect these soldiers as they discharge their duties.
Protect them with the shield of your strength
And keep them safe from all evil and harm.
May the power of your love enable them to return home
In safety, that with all who love them,
They may ever praise you for your loving care.
We ask this through Christ our Lord.

United States Conference of Catholic Bishops

★ ★ ★

★ ⭐ ★

_____

_____

_____

_____

_____

_____

_____

_____

_____

_____

_____

_____

_____

_____

_____

_____

_____

_____

_____

_____

_____

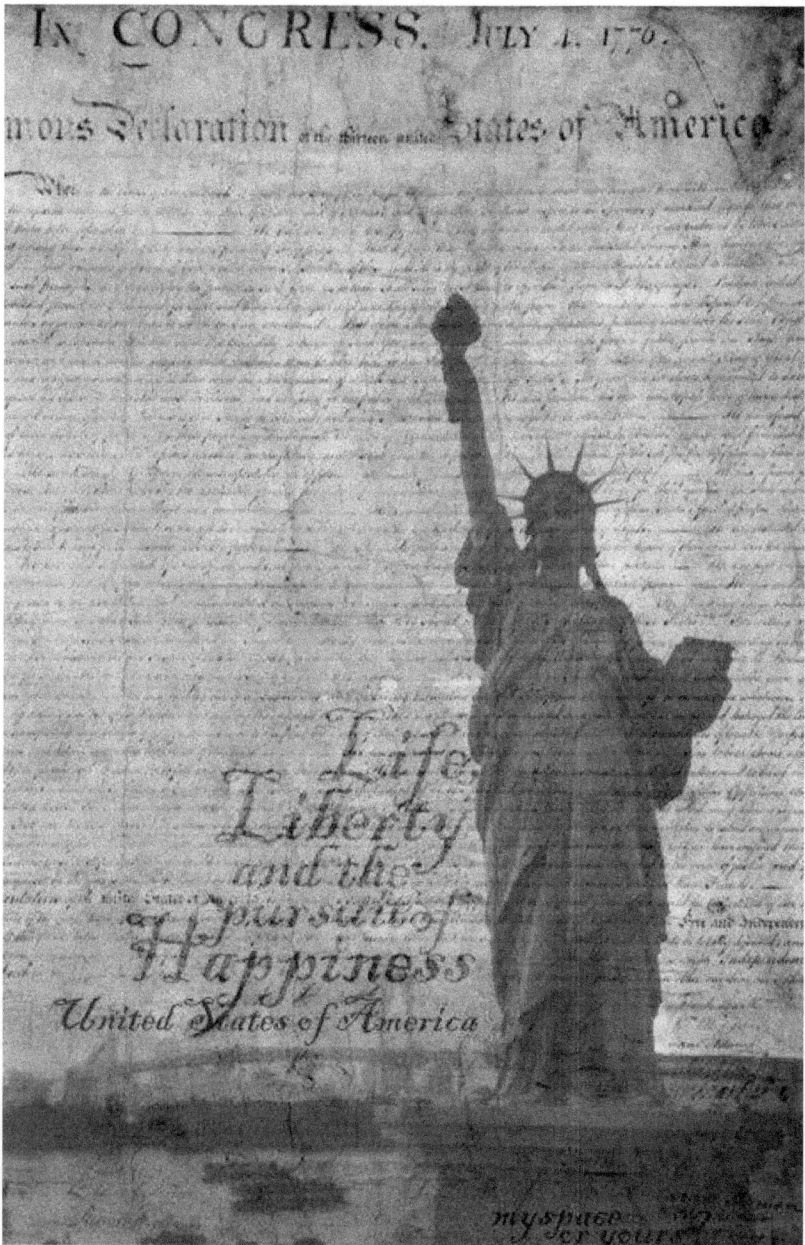

A Message in the Stars

My mama had to go to war
And this is what she said,
"Look out your window in the night
Before you go to bed

And when you see the twinkling stars
There dancing high above
Believe they're little angels and
They're sending you my love

For every lovely angel holds
A candle with a light
That fills the wind with words of love
And makes the darkness bright

And if you listen to the wind
You'll hear her gently say,
"Your mama's coming home real soon,
She's surely on the way."

So get into your downy quilt
And rest your precious head
The stars will send you words of love
The wind will rock your bed

And when you wake to greet the day
When all the stars are gone
Smile your sweetest smile for me
'Cause mama's coming home!"

Kate Watkins Furman

My Dad

My dad is my hero
He is the one I look up to
No matter what he does, he does no wrong
Now he is leaving got Iraq for a year and a half
I will not see him for so long
I fear the worse that may come
I may never see my dad again
But my dad is a fighter and he will always be
In my heart no matter what
He may be just in spirit
He may be just by phone
He may just by letters
But he'll never be alone
If he doesn't come back
From serving our country
Everyone will know what happened to my dad
He will never die

He will never disappear
He will always be my hero
Whether he is far away
Or very near
My dad can walk on water
He can do anything he wants
He is fighting for our country
Doing just like he wants
He is leaving three kids behind
And so much more
But I am daddy's little girl
And to me he is much more
If there wasn't a god
I would want him to be it
My dad is so amazing
I don't know what to say
But only that he is my hero
And I love him so very much

Saundra R. Hays
(Dedicated to her father, Michael Hays)

Could It Be?

Could it be?
Another time
That's we'll meet again
When the sun's turning wheel
Bights the falling day
Could it be another time of
Second chances for us
If there is the past
To go
How could you know?
Could it be another day?
If such may be?
When the sun's turning wheel
Bights the earth indeed?
Could it be another chance of
Breaking up the time
If the time exists
To go
How could you know?
Could you be?
Just for me
For only me?
Could you know the simplest way of
Resting places away
Could you be?
Just for me
For only me?
Could it be another way of
Life among the living weapons?
Love among the loving peoples?

Irena Rojo-Horodynska

For You...

On those lonely nights
When you sit on your bed
And think of your dad
Please don't be sad

Your dad went to war
He fought a good fight
He gave his life
For what was so right

He died a hero
A man with respect
It's how he lived life
No more to expect

He didn't die alone
His friends were nearby
So don't be upset
He saved many lives

He went away
You were such a young age
His death ends a chapter
But you must turn the page

There are happier days
So many ahead
But remember your dad
And remember the dead

He'd love to see you
As your life moves on
He'll be there in spirit
So he's not really gone

These words are for you
The daughter, the son
Your life may feel empty
But it's just begun

Erik J. Ekstrom

Cool the Thunder

Cool the thunder
Continue to wonder
Don't let them plunder
Our treasures asunder

War is a greed
That we cannot heed
This is decreed
Along with the freed

Wars we are told
Are want of oil and gold
The ones who are cold
Are ruthless and bold

Keep safe our buildings
The art on the ceilings
Museums with gildings
Lead proper proceedings

Leave for generations
Places for congregations
For meetings and salutations
Along with forums and evaluations

Museums filled with treasures
Protect them with all measures
Providing man with pleasures
History and human endeavors

Ivy Kingsland

Our Heroes

My dad or my mom might not come home from this fight,
So no it's up to me to what I feel is right.
By remembering my parent and all they stood for,
I realize now how much we all lose,
When it comes to this thing called war.
When I'm all grown up, I'll want the world to understand,
About those who died on both sides of the line in the sand.
For, I hope in my lifetime to look back and say,
That in time, we all learned a less violent way
To understand on another and not to fight
To see each other in a more compassionate light.
If we can do that, the casualties across the board would be zeros,
Then all we have to do is move forward and remember our heroes.

Kevin A. Cain

Are You There?

Where are you, daddy?
Have you gone back to that place?
That horrible place.

Who took you away from us?
And put you with the other children
In the pictures?

Where are you, mommy?
We haven't smelled the kitchen smells since,
And the perfume.

Brother needs,
Sister needs to hear,
Is that you?!

Yes!

H.E.M.

Soldier's Little Girl

"Who's that man?"
A little voice asks
The picture stares
A face of masks

The man in uniform
A flag behind
Scarred face stolid
His green eyes kind

"That's your daddy."
A quiet reply
The little girl smiles
Her eyes asking why

"He fights for you, baby
He keeps you free
He loves his girl
Can't you see?"

Little fingers touch the frame
Falling across the face
A smile slowly spreads
As she remembers his embrace

Her daddy is a hero
He makes everything okay
To this little girl
He always saves the day

The soldier fights so hard
For his precious little girl
Her father is her hero
Giving her the world

Jason Webb

The Prayer of a Soldier's Child

My daddy went away to war
I'm sad because he's gone
The days are very lonesome and
The nights are very long

My mom and I, we pray each night
That he'll be safe and warm
That god will hold him near and keep
Him safe from every harm

And in my heart, I'm thankful for
The gift dad's given me
He stands for honor, fights for peace
He keeps our country free

Kate Watkins Furman

Freedom

You close your eyes, open them,
Look down left, then right, circle around,
And back the other way,
Hum the refrain
For two, count to five, finish the song.

Thinking all the while about the lines,
In your head,
You tap that point above your nose,
Inside, then outside your brow
Where thought resides,
Of lives lost, focus on that spot,
Then below your eyes, nose, lips feel
The painful part near your heart,
And under those arms that held the gun,
Thumb, middle and pinky,
Poised, karate chop, let it go,
And know,
We have the freedom to choose
Our own ending to every tale.

Laura Levendofske

Our Heroes

Name:
Relation:
Date of Birth:
Age:
Military Branch:
Rank:
Location/Stationed:
Date:

Our Heroes

Name:
Relation:
Date of Birth:
Age:
Military Branch:
Rank:
Location/Stationed:
Date:

All the Pretty Horses

Hush-a-bye don't you cry,
Go to sleep-y, little baby.
When you wake you shall have
All the pretty little horses.
Blacks and bays, dapple grays,
Coach and six white horses.
Hush-a-bye don't you cry,
Go to sleep-y, little baby.

Traditional American (Southern)

Tell Me a Story

Tell me a story,
Tell me a story,
Tell me a story,
Remember what you said,
You promised me,
You said you would,
You gotta give in so I'll be good,
Tell me a story and then I'll go to bed.

Traditional

Man is not on the earth solely for his own happiness,
He is there to realize great things for humanity.

Vincent Van Gogh

A Prayer for Those in the Military

Almighty God
We stand before you in supplication,
Asking your divine mercy and protection,
To envelop with your invincible armor,
Our loved ones in all branches of the service.

Give them courage and strength
Against all enemies,
Both spiritual and physical,
And hasten their safe journey,
Back to their families.

If it be your holy will
That they be gathered to your bosom,
With the eternal vanguard of the saints,
Let their journey to your everlasting arms
Be swift and painless,
Where they may stand in honor and glory,
Praising you for all eternity.

Amen.

A Native American Prayer for Peace

O Great Spirit of our ancestors, I raise my pipe to you.
To your messengers the four winds, and to Mother Earth who
Provides for your children:
Give us the wisdom to teach our children to love, to respect
And to be kind to each other so that they may grow with peace in
mind.
Let us learn to share all the good things that you provide for
Us on this Earth.

★ ★ ★

LET FREEDOM RING

After Everything

After everything that's happened,
After all that you've been through
It seems impossible to move on and try to start anew

Keep in mind you're not alone,
You've still got those who care,
They're the ones who'll be there for you when the pain's too much
to bear

After all your sorrow,
After all that's gone so wrong
Do your best to find some comfort,
In a friend or in a song

Remember all that's good in life,
The things that make you whole
And don't forget that things can happen,
Things that give you no control

After everything seems to be lost,
Take time to find yourself
You'll realize you can be your own best friend,
When there is no one else

Of course, you'll always have your friends,
They're locked inside your soul
But you need to find your inner strength
This has to be your goal

After the ones you love the most have been taken away
And it seems nothing can help you
There's nothing to do or say

It's then you find how strong you are,
No matter what the case
You will come through and beat this
After everything you've faced

Jaclyn Boser

War Paint Rusting

No matter how many coats
You can't paint the war
It's not yellow or gold
It's not pink or orange
It's red
It's death
Do I have to accept? War is a tiny band aid for eternal bleeding
Temporary
I won't regret
Mortuary
I won't forget
Hold my hand through the red

Calvin Markus

You Tell Me

Once upon a time
Hey, time out
This is your story
Not mine
Only you can say
What today means
In your world
Only you may say
What yesterday means
In your world
So what will you say?
How does it turn out?
Only you can say
This is your story
Not mine

Roger Wyer, Author of *Choosing Joy at Work*

Untitled

My week has been swell
Besides the fact I'm ducking from bombs
Over my head they go
I see them fall
I see them crash
Bombs not of peace but of death
I see someone in pain under fire
I see one crash
Another life abandoned
Men of brothers
Women of sisters
I see them fall
I see them crash
Another one hits
Adrenaline pumps
As I jump I crash
Another life has left

Tyler Lee Caverly

Weather or Not

What is the rain?
Where does she come from?
What is her purpose?

What is the wind?
From where does she swirl?
What is her aim, boys and girls?

And what is the snow?
What does she know to tell?
To quell our fears here?

What is the sun?
From where does her heart burn?
With reasons for of all our seasons?

Without her
The mother of our hearth
We are cold like snow that hails upon us

'Til her return in the spring
Does the ice melting thing
That softens cold into rain

Stormy tears not
Gone, fears gone warm
And on the wind swirls the tail

The message, girls and boy
We're all here if you listen
Wind, rain, snow, and sun, joys!

Weather or not
Whether or not
Love's will aims for you, won!

H.E.M.

Not Alone

I'm not alone

Although
It feels like it at times
You were always by my side
Now I forget your face sometimes

I'm not alone

And yet,
Too often I am lonely
I have to share you with the world
But what I need is you to hold me

I'm not alone

I know,
To this country you're a hero
Stationed miles and miles away
Communications close to zero

I'm not alone

For I know that you'll come back
We'll share our smiles and our laughs
There'll be no need to fade to black

I'm not alone

Trust me,
Neither are you
So many others share this story
But happy endings can come true

You're not alone

Abby Krause

Feelings

Let them out
The tears, the joy
Show your feelings
Don't be coy

Trust in yourself
That your feelings are true
Feel your emotions
We feel them too

Let them out
The happiness and sorrow
For today's another day
And then there's tomorrow

Let them flow
The smiles and the tears
They will continue
Throughout the years

Let them out
The laughs and the cries
We live on our emotions
Till we say good-bye

Erik J. Ekstrom

To Leave a Love Behind

I read the letter quietly, knowing who its from
I let her read it after, my body going numb
I force a sad smile, receive a sad sigh
Her eyes searching mine, asking and wondering why

I take her in my arms, she clings to me real tight
I whisper to her softly, "Don't worry, I'll be all right."
"I can't do this again," she mumbles into my chest.
I kiss her softly, before getting up to get dressed

I look into the mirror, see the age etched in my face
Leaving her behind, I drop my head in disgrace
I step out onto the porch, my uniform clean and on
I stare into the east, watch the night become the dawn

Her soft hands slips gently, silently into mine
We stand there in silence, our fingers intertwined
"It's time to go," she whispers, holding back her tears
"I know," I murmur back, choking back my fears

We make the trip in silence, not wanting to break down and cry
We step up to the gate, not ready to say good-bye
"Don't worry, I'll be back," my promise whispered in her ear
Her tears fall on my shoulder, her crying hard to hear

I give her one last kiss, force out my same sad smile
Turn and walk away, praying this is worthwhile
I used to know it was, I'm not so sure anymore
Leaving my love behind, and going off to war

Jason Webb

Do You See Our Victory

Do you see our victory?
Sliding down with wings?
Do you see our freedom?
Covered with green fields?

Do you see those children?
Praying on their knees?
Do you see their mothers?
Longing for the peace?

Do you know tomorrow,
Someone will die too,
For the rights and justice
For me and for you?

The roots of you father
Comes from an unknown land
But you son, speak English
And don't be behind...

Irena Rojo-Horodynska

The Morning

When I awake
I see the sun
I see the birds
I plan for fun

When you awake
You see the day
A time to fight
And disarray

When I awake
I smell the air
A beautiful fragrance
The flowers- I stare

When you awake
You check your gun
Through sandy landscape
And burning sun

When I awake
I feel secure
Because you're there
We'll all endure

Erik J. Ekstrom

Our Heroes

Name:
Relation:
Date of Birth:
Age:
Military Branch:
Rank:
Location/Stationed:
Date:

Our Heroes

Name:
Relation:
Date of Birth:
Age:
Military Branch:
Rank:
Location/Stationed:
Date:

Anchors Aweigh
The United States Navy Theme Song

Stand, Navy, out to sea, fight our battle cry,
We'll never change our course, so vicious foe
Steer shy-y-y-y.
Roll out the TNT, anchors aweigh.
Sail on to victory
And sink their bones to Davy Jones, hooray!

Anchors aweigh, my boys, anchors aweigh.
Farewell to college joys, we sail at break of day-ay-ay-ay.
Through our last night on shore, drink to the foam,
Until we meet once more,
Here's wishing you a happy voyage home.

The United States Air Force Song

Off we go into the wild blue yonder,
Climbing high into the sun,
Here they come, zooming to meet our thunder,
At 'em boys, give 'er the gun!
Down we dive, spouting our flame from under,
Off with one hell-of-a-roar!
We live in fame or go down in flame,
Nothing will stop the U.S. Air Force!

It should be our purpose in life to see that each of us makes such a contribution as will enable us to say that we, individually and collectively, are a part of the answer to the world problem and not a part of the problem itself.

Andrew Cordier

Buddhist Prayer

By the power and the truth of practice,
May all beings have happiness, and the causes of happiness.
May all be free from sorrow, and the causes of sorrow.
May all never be separated from the sacred happiness which is
sorrowless.
And may all live in equanimity,
Without too much attachment and too much aversion,
And live believing in the equality of all that lives.

May all beings be filled with joy and peace.
May all beings everywhere,
The strong and the weak,
The great and the small,
The mean and the powerful,
The short and the long,
The subtle and the gross:
May all beings everywhere,
Seen and unseen,
Dwelling far off or nearby,
Being or waiting to become:
May all be filled with lasting joy.

Let no one deceive another,
Let no one anywhere despise another,
Let no one out of anger or resentment
Wish suffering on anyone at all.
Just as a mother with her own life
Protects her child, her only child, from harm,
So within yourself let grow
A boundless love for all creatures.

Let your love flow outward through the universe,
To its height, its depth, its broad extent,
A limitless love, without hatred or enmity.
Then as you stand or walk,
Sit or lie down,
As long as you are awake,
Strive for this with a one-pointed mind,
Your life will bring heaven to earth.

Guardian Angel Prayer

Guardian angel from heaven so bright,
Watching beside me to lead me aright,
Fold thy wings around me, and guard me with love,
Softly sing songs to me of heaven above.
Amen.

★ ★ ★

★ ★ ★

_____
_____
_____
_____
_____
_____
_____
_____
_____
_____
_____
_____
_____
_____
_____
_____
_____
_____
_____
_____
_____
_____
_____

The Difference Between Us

We are not lost, and you are not forgotten
Absence of touch defines your fear
Though in your heart you know we're near
A space separates in body and mind
But soul is left with you behind
Our love is no less for you so distant
Which makes for a duty more resistant
We may see tragedy that no one should view
But the smiles on faces know we'll soon come home to you

Jeffrey Pearson

A Child of All Seasons

In the summer
A brighter sun plays
Above the darkening sky's rain

As we jump and spin
Round and round
Skating to hope our hopes not so vain

In the autumn
A shower of leaves alights
In the crisp, chilling air

As we ready,
And play our all-ready masquerade
Our hope a despair?

In the winter
The land wears a frigid frost
Of blanket whites, dark nights

As we warm
To the wish of a New Year
And wait to see wrong be right

In the spring
Comes the promise of sweet bouquets
Love on every small vine

As we strain to dance
Dance away strain of budding weeds
Water needs crime

And in the summer, winter, spring, and fall
We all watch, eager
Wait, wait…

H.E.M.

Why I Still Cry

On my left,
Fiery flames in my head
On my right,
My own death instead

Village children,
Little hands outstretched
Comrades fallen,
Faces forever etched

In my mind they hide,
Side by side, without fail
Not above or below,
At that fork in the trail

Laura Levendofske

The Lady of the Harbor

My mama got the news today
That daddy died at war
The sadness that has touched our lives
We've never known before
But mama said not to be sad
He died a hero's death
Democracy and freedom are
The precious gifts he left
And the lady of the harbor
Holds high the endless flame
That floods the world with freedom's light
And burns in daddy's name

Kate Watkins Furman

Love Goes On

Your life is facing changes, ones you might not understand.
I gets so tough to face the world, but you know you can.

So when you're feeling left out, that you really don't belong
There's something you should hold onto: Love goes on.

Through days filled up with sadness, your sorrow goes so deep
To nights where you just lay there, and cry yourself to sleep

It's hard, it's unfair, and it feels so very wrong
But try your hardest to remember, love goes on

Everyone seems happy, nothing drags them down
They're all filled up with smiles, nobody ever frowns

So if you ever start to feel like you're a tagalong
The thing that you must tell yourself is simple: Love goes on

Love goes on in so many ways that seem too strange to be real
It's not something that we can see, something we only feel

Love goes on forever, it'll be there 'til the end
Keep that in mind when you feel you don't have a single friend

Love goes on because it's powerful and never can be broken
Love is something that you do, it's not something that's spoken

Love is something beautiful, so hard to come across
But if you still believe in it, it never can be lost

So keep in mind that even when someone you love is gone
They're still there looking out for you because their love goes on

Jaclyn Boser

That Fateful Day

On that fateful day,
When nine months had passed,
It was time to bring new life
Into this world at long last.

The labor was long,
The pain was excruciating,
But when the angel handed to her,
The new born baby, the pain was gone.

As she gazed at the tiny being,
She gasped with awe,
While weeping with joy,
She fell in love, deeper than she'd ever known.

Rev. Andrea Boyungs

Your Endless Chapter

The sun flexes its sun beams
Highlights our lives
At the darkest times
We felt the same rays
When I was warm
You were cold
You were warm
Halfway around the world
You're still around the corner
Your hand is still on my shoulder
I won't shake
If life is a play
Yours had endless applause
An endless ovation
You are in the sun
I see you every day
I hold hands with your sun rays
At last
Warm together
Your endless chapter

Calvin Markus

Always Here Now

Remember that hug?
Close your eyes
Go there now
Feel it again!
Remember that laugh?
Close your eyes
Go there now
Hear it again!
Remember the way they smell?
Close your eyes
Go there now
Fill you up with that smell!
Open your eyes
Look at you
See the piece of them
Always here now

Roger Wyer

On the Land and On Our Sorrows

On the horizon the helicopters swoon
Creating a shadow the light of the moon
Visions of war casting a gloom
On the land and on our sorrows

People and places surrounding our world
How we would help them if only we could
We must remember that there's always good
On the land and on our sorrows

A calling upon us as we cry and weep
The lessons and values that we try to keep
Holding steadfast as we sink in the deep
On the land and on our sorrows

If be our choice we would always have peace
The wars of the world…they would all cease
The number of brothers they now decrease
On the land and on our sorrows

The war in which we find ourselves…could there be an end?
The horror and the aftermath we will have to mend
These thoughts we think as we fight and defend
On the land and on our sorrows

Above all of our lives the sun begins to rise
Shining the light as we lift up our eyes
A new hope is dawning and no more good-byes
On the land and on our sorrows

Ivy Kingsland

Untitled #2

As I sit there wondering
Wondering if daddy will come home
Come home someday
Someday daddy will come home

I remember it as if it was yesterday, as I looked up
Looking into his eyes saying to myself, "Daddy don't go!"
As I thought that I knew
I just know he will be fine and we will too

But daddy had to
He had to go
I miss him, I miss him very much
But I know he will return

1 year, 3 months, and 19 days
He came home
I saw him get off the plane I knew
I knew we were okay

Tyler Lee Caverly

Our Heroes

Name:
Relation:
Date of Birth:
Age:
Military Branch:
Rank:
Location/Stationed:
Date:

Our Heroes

Name:
Relation:
Date of Birth:
Age:
Military Branch:
Rank:
Location/Stationed:
Date:

The Marines Hymn

From the halls of Montezuma
To the shores of Tripoli
We will fight out county's battles
In the air, on land, and sea.
First to fight for right and freedom
And to keep our honor clean,
We are proud to claim the title
United States Marine.
Our flag's unfurled to every breeze
From dawn to setting sun,
We have fought in every clime and place
Where we could take a gun.
In the snow of far-off northern lands
And in the sunny tropic scenes,
You will find us always on the job—
The United States Marines.
Here's health to you and your corps
Which we are proud to serve,
In many a strife we've fought for life
And never lost our nerve.
If the Army and the Navy
Ever look on Heaven's scenes,
They will find the streets guarded
By United States Marines.

The Army Goes Rolling Along
The official United States Army theme song
Based on "The Caissons Go Rolling Along"

March along, sing our song, with the Army of the free
Count the brave, count the true, who have fought to victory
We're the Army and proud of our name
We're the Army and proudly proclaim

First to fight for the right,
And to build the nation's might,
And the Army goes rolling along
Proud of all we have done,
Fighting till the battle's won,
And the Army goes rolling along.

Then it's Hi! Hi! Hey!
The Army's on its way.
Count off the cadence loud and strong (Two! Three!)
For where e'er we go,
You will always know
That the Army goes rolling along.

Valley Forge, Custer's ranks,
San Juan Hill and Patton's tanks,
And the Army went rolling along
Minute men, from the start,
Always fighting from the heart,
And the Army keeps rolling along.

When you get into a tight place and everything goes against you, till it seems as though you could not hang on a minute longer, never give up then, for that is just the place and time that the tide will turn.

Harriet Beecher Stowe

Make Me an Instrument of Your Peace
Saint Francis Prayer

Lord, make me an instrument of your peace.
Where there is hatred, let me sow love,
Where there is injury, pardon,
Where there is doubt, faith,
Where there is despair, hope,
Where there is darkness, light,
Where there is sadness, joy.
O Divine Master,
Grant that I may not so much seek to be consoled as to console,
To be understood as to understand,
To be loved as to love,
For it is the giving that we receive,
It is in dying that we are born again in eternal life.

She Who Heals
An American Indian Healing Prayer

Mother, sing me a song
That will ease my pain,
Mend broken bones,
Bring wholeness again.
Catch my babies
When they are born,
Sing my death song,
Teach me how to mourn.
Show me the medicine
Of the healing herbs,
The value of spirit,
The way I can serve.
Mother, heal my heart
So that I can see
The gifts of yours
That can live through me.

★ ★ ★

★ ★ ★

★ ★ ★

_____
_____
_____
_____
_____
_____
_____
_____
_____
_____
_____
_____
_____
_____
_____
_____
_____
_____
_____
_____
_____
_____
_____
_____
_____

Untitled

Mama, where did daddy go?
He went off to war
He got the call three weeks ago
He's going into the Corps

He'll train all day
And through the night
To win the war
And to win the fight

But daddy said he wouldn't leave again
I'm sorry but that's not true
He's going to restore democracy
He's going for me and you

What to do if he doesn't come home?
What if my daddy dies?
Just know that he will always be here
In your smiles and your cries

Your daddy's been trained
The best he can
He'll be protected
He's a blessed man

He cares for you
And he cares for me
Your daddy will be safe
As you will soon see

In eighteen months
He'll walk through the door
Then your daddy's not leaving anymore

Your daddy's not leaving anymore!

Erik J. Ekstrom

Soldier Daddy

To you I may be very small
Or think I don't know much at all
I've learned to grow rather fast
With so much future and not much past

I'm just two years old but often sad
I want so much to hug my dad
He's protecting us from far away
His life on the line every day

I watch my mom and see her cry
I already know but still ask why?
Her heart is hurting yet she tries to smile
And we hold each other for a little while

I'm still young yet very wise
I have my fun but realize
My soldier daddy is brave and strong
I pray his deployment won't be long

Gina M. Makowsky

Army Man

Mother, I'm so sorry
He is not a delinquent
All girls have their boyfriends
And I feel so different

Mother, please forgive me
I am not so little
I am almost a woman
And want to have some title

Mother, I was waiting
Sixteen long years
Let me be an adult
Don't show me your tears

Yes, he will protect me
He is an Army man
Don't you see I love him?
Don't you understand?

Don't worry I ask you
Don't be crying, Mother
Cause I never told you
He reminds me of Father

Irena Rojo-Horodynska

Green Bag

Mommy was wearing an all blue uniform,
Carrying a big green bag on her back
On the day we dropped her off,
Her ship was heading to Iraq
She kept hugging me and saying, "I love you, my little man,"
As we stood outside the gate
Daddy was very quiet standing there
I could see the tears rolling down his face

The floating ship was the biggest thing I had ever seen
A huge banner read "Good Luck, Big John!"
As if waved in the cold ocean breeze
There were so many people dressed in blue
Carrying boxes, bags, and food
I even saw a few small planes
Like the ones my grandpa flew

Mommy said it was time to go and she would see us around the
end of May
I told her I would be her strong "Little Man"
And I'd write to her each and every day
Daddy gave us all a big bear hug
And told Mommy everything would be just fine
We'd send her favorite cookies and make cards
The giant heart one would be mine

As mommy climbed the stairs
She turned to us with a big smile and waved
And when she faced the American flag
I thought she looked so brave
That wasn't the first time
I had to say good-bye and I know why mommy had to leave
Because just like grandpa
She wants me to be happy and free

Irene Lowe

Brother, I Thank You for...

Your tears when I fell of my first bike,
Laughing when I lost your best knife,
Holding up my head those times I got sick,
Careful excuses at school when I skipped.

Pulling me to shore, though you couldn't swim,
Taking seriously my most fantastic whims,
Refusing to leave when I told you to go,
When I asked for too much, telling me no.

Needing less when I had little to give,
Dying so bravely you taught me to live.

Laura Levendofske

The American eagle

Great masterpiece, unfurl your wings
Soaring where the water sings
Blue heaven touches earth below
Where fruitful fields and flowers grow

Where wars, now past, have set us free
Sweet symbol of our liberty
Fly on, fly on, your strength increase
God lift you up on winds of peace

Kate Watkins Furman

Keep Smiling

It's tough to feel so sad, like your happiness is gone.
It seems you'll never be able to smile and move on.

It seems your life is over now, the good parts anyway.
You wonder if it's worth it to get out of bed each day.

Just know, this is the hardest that your life will ever be.
Keep that in mind while wondering, "Tell me, please, why me?"

Life is full of tests to see how strong we really are.
Yours is so very difficult, surpasses most by far.

So when it tries to overtake you, just hold your head up high.
Show your smile to the world, but don't forget to cry.

Be proud of what your parents did, don't let it be in vain.
It was such a sacrifice, it filled you up with pain.

It's a must to show your feelings, whatever they may be.
You can smile, you can cry, you can laugh, you can be free.

But when sadness has you feeling trapped, and like you can't
escape.
Turn that frown upside down, and smile for your own sake.

For if you feel alone, like you're your own best friend.
Keep in mind that that's not true, the memories never end.

Keep them in your heart and soul, those parts are great for filing!
And when you bring them out to see, I know that you'll keep
smiling.

Jaclyn Boser

Anthony

Peals of laughter sing through the air
As I kiss your precious little tummy
You grab hold of my hair
Tiny little hands
Cute little toes
Flail and wave
Ouch! You got me on my nose
Slobber, drool, and milk aplenty
My boy, what joy you bring to me!

Rev. Andrea Boyungs

Hey Kid

You're not alone
You're not the only one
Who ever played
This game before
You're not alone
At just this moment
Everywhere through time
Someone is missing
You're not alone
At just this moment
Everywhere through time
Someone is found
You're not alone
At just this moment
Everywhere through time
Everyone is holding hands

Roger Wyer

A Mask for an Ugly War

If only there was a mirror big enough
So the war could see how ugly it is
As truth is left locked in its room
The key is swallowed along with you
You can't heal a wound with a bullet
I'll find you
I'll save you
Whether or not you're coming home
I'll find your ghost
The cities, the mountains
Anywhere you want to go
The world is ours
Our home
The world to roam

Calvin Markus

God Bless America

Our Heroes

Name:
Relation:
Date of Birth:
Age:
Military Branch:
Rank:
Location/Stationed:
Date:

Our Heroes

Name:
Relation:
Date of Birth:
Age:
Military Branch:
Rank:
Location/Stationed:
Date:

Then it's Hi! Hi! Hey!
The Army's on its way.
Count off the cadence loud and strong (Two! Three!)
From where e'er we go,
You will always know
That the Army goes rolling along.

Men in rags, men who froze,
Still that Army met its foes,
And the Army went rolling along.
Faith in God, then we're right,
And we'll fight with all our might,
As the Army keeps rolling along.

Then it's Hi! Hi! Hey!
The Army's on its way.
Count off the cadence loud and strong (Two! Three!)
For where e'er we go,
You will always know
That the Army goes rolling along.

Brigadier General E.L. Gruber

My Country 'Tis of Thee

My country tis of thee,
Sweet land of liberty,
Of thee I sing.
Land where my fathers died!
Land of the Pilgrim's pride!
From every mountain side,
Let freedom ring!

My native country, thee,
Land of the noble free,
Thy name I love.
I love thy rocks and rills,
Thy woods and templed hills;
My heart with rapture fills
Like that above.

Let music swell the breeze,
And ring from all the trees
Sweet freedom's song.
Let mortal tongues awake;
Let all that breathe partake;
Let rocks their silence break,
The sound prolong.

Our father's God to, Thee,
Author of liberty,
To Thee we sing.
Long may our land be bright
With freedom's holy light;
Protect us by Thy might,
Great God, our King!

Samuel Francis Smith

This country was not built by men who relied on someone else to take care of them. It was built by men who relied on themselves, who dared to shape their own lives, who had enough courage to blaze their own trails- enough confidence in themselves to take the necessary risks.

J. Ollie Edmunds

Do not believe in what you have heard. Do not believe traditions because they have been handed down for many generations. Do not believe anything because it is rumored and spoken of many. Do not believe merely because the written statement of some old sage is produced. Do not believe in conjectures. Do not believe merely in the authority of your teachers and elders. After observation and analysis, when it agrees with reason and is conducive to the good and benefit of one and all, then accept it and live up to it.

Buddha

Prayer for the Act of Hope

O my God, relying on your infinite goodness and promises, I hope to obtain pardon of my sins, the help of your grace and the life everlasting, through the merits of Jesus Christ, my Lord and Redeemer.

★ ⭐ ★

_____

_____

_____

_____

_____

_____

_____

_____

_____

_____

_____

_____

_____

_____

_____

_____

_____

_____

_____

_____

_____

_____

_____

★ ★ ★

"The clustered stars
and the steadfast bars,
The red, the white,
and the blue!"

War Is

War is a trial
That takes loves ones away
War is a battlefield
Where no one wants to stay

War is started by governments
Want to have their way
War is not righteous
At the end of the day

War is a price
In which many have to pay
War is an explosion
That should be kept at bay

Ivy Kingsland

Waiting

I miss you, mom
You're so far away
In another country
And yet you still stay

I try to sleep
But you're on my mind
A mission of peace
You're trying to find

Some say you kill
Some say it's not right
But I am proud
You're an angel of light

You are a medic
You're on the front lines
You don't kill, you save
Some don't see the signs

An angel of mercy
Taking care of them all
I've tried your phone
But you don't answer the call

I know you are busy
I just need to hear
That you are all right
And to feel you near

Mom, I am waiting
For you to arrive
Please come back home
Make it back to me alive

Mom, I am waiting
Waiting…
Waiting…

Erik J. Ekstrom

Untitled #3

As I look in the sky
Wishing to fly
Fly to my mom
Fly away, far, far away just to see

In order to fly
I must believe
Believe I can
To see my mom again

All that has been accomplished is believing
Believing that I'll soar with her
Nothing happening, only dreaming
Dreaming of that day

That day she'll be
She'll be in my arms
That day comes
I'm soaring in the air because I'm in her arms

Tyler Lee Caverly

Sunday

"Hi, Jennifer, you look nice."

"Thanks."

"Where ya goin'?"

"Nowhere."

"Oh, then, um…why're ya?"

"Church."

"But, you said--"

"I know, I like putting on these clothes, like I used to when…"

"Uh, hey it's Sunday and there's no school tomorrow, also, so wanna come over, I got Madden 09 and XBOX 360 O Lite, an..."

"Billy, do you ever pray?"

"Sure, sometimes when I want stuff to happen, ya know?"

"Thanks Billy, maybe we can play later, I have to go now."

"Um, okay, Jen, then…"

"We can play later."

H.E.M.

For Love of Our Country

Whether it's Army, Navy, Air Force, or Marines,
The men and women in service protect your rights
For some, it's a job, for others, it's a dream

Those in the military put their lives in danger
They're willing to do things that most of us wouldn't do
They'll lay down their lives and die for a perfect stranger
How many people do you know who would do that for you?

Nobody enlists with the hope of going to war,
But they're well aware that someday they may have to
You, as an American, have lots to be thankful for
Next time you see someone in uniform, say, "Thank you."

As a country, we to back these women and men,
And give them our respect and tell them that we're proud
They leave their families for tours time and time again
Let's pray for their safe return together and out loud.

P.J. Scheidel

The military is doing their best
Fighting for our country every single day
They go where they're needed, whether east or west
Because of them, our freedom is here to stay

Joseph Scheidel
(Age 7- 2008)

When the Wind Blows Softly

The other side is not some place
A million miles up there in space
Only one who's passed over knows
We progress like a blooming rose
Never rushing, never pushing, they unfurl
Patiently waiting for each petal to uncurl
Only to become exactly what's meant to be
It's individual beauty, only time can see
There's a purpose to life, no matter how brief
Even if it's not clear and we feel extreme grief
The imperishable influence they had on our life
God's marionette, they did pilgrim invariable strife
And it's my comfort in knowing that,
My mom, God did not take
For I know that his heart was the first to break
It was all in the plan, for my dear loved one
Time to pass, when all worldly work is done
Dear loved one, I see your portrait in the clouds above
Your whimsical understanding, unconditional love
When the wind blows softly, it will carry a kiss
It's your laughter, your hugs, your worldly presence I'll miss

Pamala Kim Everts

My Brother

I am so very proud
Of how he turned out to be
He is out there standing his ground
Fighting for our country
I could not ask for a better man
To be in my family
I am glad God had this plan
For me to a brother like thee
We may not have got along
And we may have had our fights
But we turned out to be strong
And stand up for what is right
We got raised by the best
And I know my brother will agree
They put us to the test
To make sure we could be all we could be
I just want my brother to know
That deep down in my heart
There is a special glow
That gets bigger when we're apart
It is a glow of love for you
That cannot be explained
And it will go through
Anything that gets in its way
So just remember this
That I am always here
And I will always wish
That we will always be near

Virginia Thom

I Wish I Were a Kid Again

I wish I were a small kid again
Not to think more than I'm suppose to
And ever look to find out things
About to those I'm even close to

I wish I never grew so fast
Running outside the house and whistle
Carrying in hands this funny toy
That turned to be one day a pistol

I wish I closed my eyes before
The day I came to see my mother
I wish I never saw this war
And never knew who was my father

I wish I don't know everything
Not question when and how and why
Excusing those who got to win
Remembering those who choose to die

Irena Rojo-Horodynska

The Ride Home

I snuggle down into your favorite chair
Brown leather, big enough to hold me,
Reading books about bombers, submarines.
Whirl the rocker round, dizzy with longing,
Imagine you running fast, across the white sand,
Follow intersecting lines across the lighted globe
That sits on a table by our front door,
I trace routes that could bring you home.

Laura Levendofske

Our Heroes

Name:
Relation:
Date of Birth:
Age:
Military Branch:
Rank:
Location/Stationed:
Date:

Our Heroes

Name:
Relation:
Date of Birth:
Age:
Military Branch:
Rank:
Location/Stationed:
Date:

Rock-A-Bye, Baby

Rock-a-bye baby,
On the treetop,
When the wind blows
The cradle will rock,
When the bough breaks
The cradle will fall,
And down will come baby,
Cradle and all.

Rock-a-bye, baby,
Your cradle is green,
Father's a king
And mother's a queen,
Sister's a lady
And wears a gold ring,
Brother's a drummer,
And plays for the King.

Rock-a-bye, baby,
Way up on high,
Never mind baby,
Mother is nigh,
Up to the ceiling,
Down to the ground,
Rock-a-bye, baby,
Up hill and down.

Traditional English

Toora, Loora, Loora

Toora, loora, loora,
Oh toora, looralie,
Toora, loora, loora,
Hush now, don't you cry.

Toora, loora, loora,
Oh toora, looralie,
Toora, loora, loora,
That's an Irish lullaby.

Traditional Irish

It doesn't take great men to do things,
But it is doing things that makes men great.

Arnold Glasgow

Prayer of Solace

May Crist support us all the day long,
Till the shadows lengthen,
And the evening comes,
And the busy world is hushed,
And the fever of life is over,
And our work is done,
Then in his mercy,
May he give us a safe lodging,
And holy rest and peace at last.

Amen.

(Attributed to John Cardinal Newman)

Prayer in Times of Danger

O God, who knowest us to be set in the midst of such great perils,
that, by reason of the weakness of our nature, we cannot stand
upright, grant us such health of mind and body, that those evils
which we suffer for our sins we may overcome through thine
assistance through Christ our Lord.

Amen.

★ ★ ★

_____
_____
_____
_____
_____
_____
_____
_____
_____
_____
_____
_____
_____
_____
_____
_____
_____
_____
_____
_____
_____

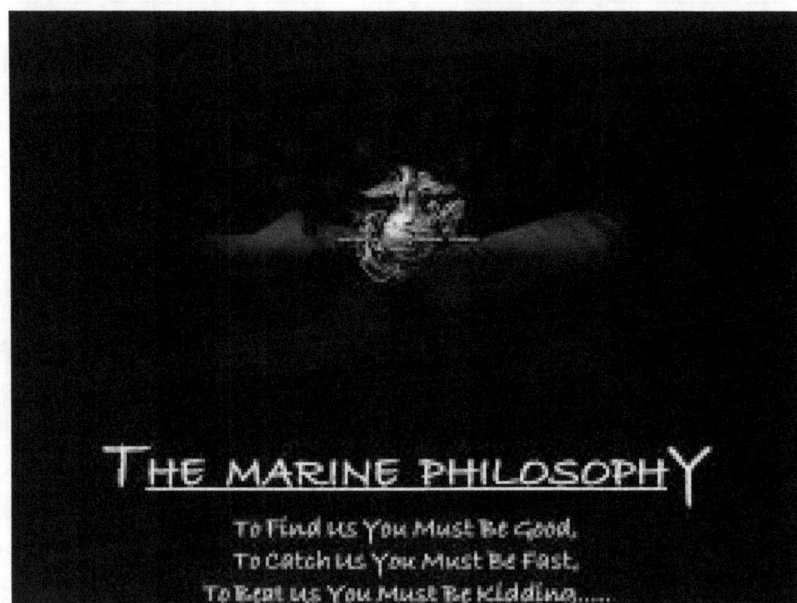

THE MARINE PHILOSOPHY

To Find us You Must Be Good,
To Catch us You Must Be Fast,
To Beat us You Must Be Kidding.....

Coming Home

My child, you were born
While I was away
Now you are two
Happy Birthday

I missed your first
And I cried all night
I looked at your pictures
What a beautiful sight

The smile on your face
And your big blue eyes
Made me feel such emotion
A sorrowful night full of cries

My pals who are here
Helped me get through the strain
The heartfelt pride
And the unbearable pain

I can't wait to hold you
In my arms so tight
To come back to you
Leave this horrible fight

I'll play with your fingers
And I'll tickle your feet
I'll be home soon
So we'll finally meet

I am your daddy
I'm home from the war
The cab will pull up
And I'll walk through the door

I'll give you a kiss
I'll be there right away
I'll never leave you again
And I promise to stay

Erik J. Ekstrom

A Brother's Dream

My brother went away to war
He's eighteen and I'm ten
I never knew that when he left
He's not come home again

And now my mother wears a star
A star made out of gold
It's something just to honor Jeff
For her to have and hold

Now every time I see the flag
My heart is filled with pride
Was for her bars of red and white
My brother fought and died

And when I've grown much older
It is a dream of mine
To take my gun and guard that flag
And watch old glory shine

Kate Watkins Furman

Still There

It's hard to lose a loved one
All you want to do is cry
Every day is dark
And you just want to know why

It's hard to feel like you're alone
But you've still got your friends
They'll always stand beside you
They'll be there 'til it ends

It's hard to laugh and play again
To still feel like a kid
You might feel like you should grow up
And do what your parents did

It's hard to feel so different
Like nobody understands
But they're still there to help you
Just reach out and take their hands

It's hard to feel so angry
And you know it's just not fair
But let them live inside your heart
And they will still be there

Jaclyn Boser

Briana

Long silken strands, spun like gold
Cinnamon sprinkling on a button nose
Peridot gems twinkle with glee
Mischievous thoughts while she watches me
A gymnast and a dancer all pulled together
With a grace to outshine the lightest feather
Quick with wit and innocent with age
Boy, is she going to be a handful when she gets to the next stage

Rev. Andrea Boyungs

The Call

It's Six AM
The alarm clock rings
The sun comes up
And the song bird sings
I get ready for work
And I'm on my way
This was my dream
Just the other day

I'm in the war
So far, far away
I signed up
Nothing more to say
I did it for my country
I did it for all
There was no stopping me
I answered the call

I've seen a difference
With the boots on the ground
We're helping a country
To be safe and sound
I miss my folks
I miss my family and friends
But I'll continue to fight
Till the bitter end

It's Six AM
The alarm clock rings
The sun comes up
And the song bird sings
I get ready for work
And I'm on my way
This was reality
When I returned today

Erik J. Ekstrom

What the Heck

You might as well
Choose joy
Or maybe you'd rather
Be angry

You can choose joy
In an instant
Or you might rather
Choose fear

Reach out
Grab that joy
Unless you prefer
Sadness

Joy needs a friend
Just like you
What the heck
Choose joy

Roger Wyer

Remember?

"Hey, Jennie, do ya wanna come over, I got the new *Atomic Robot Dogs of War*?"

"What's that?"

"Oh, it's so cool, just about my best favorite comics!"

"Is that the thing you read in school?"

"Oh sure, every day!"

"I'm reading something too…"

"Oh cool, what?"

"Ya wanna come over?"

"Sure, I'll bring--"

"No! We'll read mine."

"Okay, what's it called?"

"Chicken Little."

"Ohhh, Jennie, I know that, that's a baby's book, it's…"

"Billy, chunks of sky *are* falling!"

H.E.M.

Kacy

With impishness and innocence
She bounds through life

A shining face with bright blue eyes
A little pixie smile that's sweeter than pie

Blessed with beauty and love
She spreads her joy like the wings of a dove

With love and discipline she is raised
Her parents lift their voices with thanks and praise

Rev. Andrea Boyungs

Untitled

Very far away
Here we are at home
And east is where they stay
Their souls are with us
Their dreams hold steady
Dreams full of hope
With their minds at the ready
Fearing not for themselves
But worrying of loved ones
We hold hands over our hearts
They hold their guns
To protect our lives
Our hopes, dreams, our freedom
To hold onto our honor
We will always need them

Anthony Marceau

School Daze

"Hi, Jennifer! Are ya goin' to school today?"

"No."

"Hey, Columbus Day isn't 'til Monday?"

"Yes."

"Then, uh, why?"

"School is closed."

"Um, c'mon Jennie, they never close, even in a snowstorm right?"

"Right! But they have no more money."

"What d'ya mean no--"

"For teachers, an' books, an' lunches, an' supplies...it's all gone away and nobody knows when it's comin' back, just like from that place with the wrong spelling, no 'U' after Iraq."

H.E.M.

Our Heroes

Name:
Relation:
Date of Birth:
Age:
Military Branch:
Rank:
Location/Stationed:
Date:

Our Heroes

Name:
Relation:
Date of Birth:
Age:
Military Branch:
Rank:
Location/Stationed:
Date:

Twinkle, Twinkle Little Star

Twinkle, twinkle, little star
How I wonder what you are!
Up above the world so high,
Like a diamond in the sky.
Twinkle, twinkle, little star,
How I wonder what you are.

When the blazing sun is gone,
When the nothing shines upon,
Then you show your little light,
Twinkle, twinkle, all the night.
Twinkle, twinkle, little star,
How I wonder what you are.

Then the trav'ler in the dark,
Thanks you for your tiny spark.
He could not see which way to go,
If you did not twinkle so.
Twinkle, twinkle, little star,
How I wonder what you are.

In the dark blue sky you keep,
Often through my curtains peep.
For you never shut your eye,
Till the sun is in the sky.
Twinkle, twinkle, little star,
How I wonder what you are.

Jane Taylor (1783-1824)

God Bless America

God bless America
Land that I love
Stand beside her, and guide her
Through the night with a light from above
From the mountains
To the prairies
To the oceans white with foam
God bless America
My home, sweet home
God bless America
My home, sweet home

Irving Berlin

Evening Praise

All praise to you, O God, this night
For all the blessings of the light,
Keep us, we pray, O King of Kings,
Beneath you own almighty wings.

Forgive us, Lord, through Christ your son,
Whatever wrong this day we've done,
Your peace give to the world, O Lord,
That we might live in one accord.

Enlighten us, O Blessed Light,
And give us rest throughout this night.
O strengthen us, that for your sake,
We all may serve you when we wake.

Saint Michael
For Personal Protection

Saint Michael, the archangel! Glorious prince, chief and champion of the heavenly hosts, guardian of the souls of men, conqueror of the rebel angels! How beautiful art thou, in thy heaven-made armor. We love thee, dear prince of heaven! We, thy happy clients, yearn to enjoy thy special protection. Obtain for us from God a share of thy sturdy courage, pray that we may have a strong and tender love for our redeemer and, in every danger or temptation, be invincible against the enemy of our souls. O standard-bearer of our salvation! Be with us in our last moments and when our souls quit this earthly exile, carry them safely to the judgment seat of Christ, and may our Lord and Master bid thee bear us speedily to the Kingdom of Eternal Bliss. Teach us ever to repeat the sublime cry: "Who is like unto God?" Amen.

★ ★ ★

_____

_____

_____

_____

_____

_____

_____

_____

_____

_____

_____

_____

_____

_____

_____

_____

_____

_____

_____

★ ★ ★

_____
_____
_____
_____
_____
_____
_____
_____
_____
_____
_____
_____
_____
_____
_____
_____
_____
_____
_____
_____
_____

ALABAMA ALASKA ARIZONA ARKANSAS
CALIFORNIA COLORADO CONNECTICUT
DELAWARE FLORIDA IDAHO INDIANA IOWA
GEORGIA HAWAII KANSAS KENTUCKY
LOUISIANA MAINE MARYLAND MASSACHUSETTS
MICHIGAN MINNESOTA MISSISSIPPI
MISSOURI MONTANA NEBRASKA
NEVADA NEW HAMPSHIRE NEW JERSEY NEW MEXICO NEW YORK
NORTH CAROLINA NORTH DAKOTA OHIO OKLAHOMA OREGON
PENNSYLVANIA RHODE ISLAND SOUTH CAROLINA SOUTH DAKOTA
SOUTH DAKOTA TENNESSEE TEXAS UTAH VERMONT VIRGINIA
WASHINGTON WEST VIRGINIA WISCONSIN WYOMING

Untitled

Oh dear child
Have no fear
This world is wide
But your father is here
There is no reason to run and hide
Do me one thing
Relax and find peace
While I'm here in the Middle East
Oh how I miss you
I sure do
Oh so much, if you only knew
God bless you son
I'll be home soon

Matt Imbordino

War: I Am Behind the Curtain

If truth means we be golden fish freed,
Waves of synchronized intent,
Purpose made transparent.
Does certainty allow for freedom?

Aware servitude, such a pleasant fall,
To embrace pure instinct, does matter
Resonate, if the tune written is but enjoyed?

Can just knowledge employed,
Give choice a simpler label, war,
Or does the naming but diminish peace.

Laura Levendofske

Father to Son

Oh my little one
Tucked in tight
Nice and safe
While I'm off to fight

Don't be afraid
And don't you cry
I'll be home soon
I'm not going to die

Be strong for your mom
Be brave as can be
Take care of your sis
You're the man of the house, see?

I put you in charge
My brave little son
I put my faith in you
You are the one

Do what you can
Do what is right
And I'll return soon
From this horrible fight

But if I cannot
I want you to see
Our blood runs deep
You're a part of me

I'm so very proud
I'm proud of you all
But I've done my duty
And answered the call
I did what was right
I did it for you
My brave little boy
I love you

Erik J. Ekstrom

Be Proud

Be proud of your mom and daddy
And try to understand
They're doing this for you
And for those across our land

You know those pretty songs we sing
To show our nation's pride
Like 'My Country 'Tis of Thee'
Make us feel good inside

It's because we're proud to live here
Proud to know that we are free
Your mom and dad are fighting
To bring peace to you and me

I know how much you miss them
And how hard this is for you
But just think about wanting
To come home and be with you

Be proud of mom and daddy
Be peaceful like a dove
And remember that they're doing this
To show us all their love

Jaclyn Boser

Untitled

When a man decided to do something
He must go all the way
But he must take responsibility
For what he does
He must know first
Why he is doing it
And then must proceed with his actions
With no doubts or remorse

Carlos Castaneda

The Last Children

"Billy? Do you know about wars?"

"Sure Jennie, I know all about them."

"Tell me what you know?"

"Sure, they're cool, even though some people get killed sometimes. But I heard my dad say, 'We always gotta be ready,' then I got my Playstation Army Men: Air Attack 2."

"Billy, real people die and when one war ends there's always another to take its place, and when real people die, their families get hurt too and we cry that they're all gone..."

H.E.M.

In My Dreams

In my dreams
Night by night
Some person appears
Guessing who
That can be
Causes me some tears
I'm not sure
But I think
That stranger I see
Looks like someone
So familiar
Someone known to me

I found out this one day
While my mom was cooking
That this guy, looks the same
As my dad was looking

I asked mom
And she said,
"That may be the truth,
That your dad
In your dreams
Is coming to you."

She said,
"Son when you'll grow
You will be like him
And next time
When he comes
Tell him in your dream

That you are just as brief
As he was that day
When he left
To the war
And did not return…"

Irena Rojo-Horodynska

The Veteran

I saw him in the park, one day,
His legs had both been torn away
And in his chair, alone, he sat
In ragged coat and woolen hat.

Some shunned him as a sad disgrace
But when I'd seen that beaten face
I knew he sat there, just for me
That I might live in liberty.

For me, it was, he shed his tears
And forfeit all his youthful years
He was there when I turned to go
The tallest man I'll ever know!

Kate Watkins Furman

Untitled

Bow to me, you minions of the monkey bars!
For, I have sacrificed my father, on the alter of your freedom.
I am six years old, and they say I do not truly understand,
But I understand the most important of these many meanings.
I understand that this bicycle,
The bike he rode when I rode mine behind him
Side by side down our safe cul-de-sac street
Now sits empty, leaning against the carport wall.
Never will he ride it beside me again
Never will the wind of his movement chase his short hairs across
his scalp
His laughter is silenced forever
He will never tickle me again
Bow to me, you miserable swine!
Your parents are cowards, weaklings, fools
Incapable of knowing when their families need to be defended.
But this was not my father, he knew.
He acted, while your parents slept,
He kept them safe through the night,
And you as well, in your parents' stead.
You must be miserable to have their arms about you in evening.
Your skin must crawl when they tuck you into bed,
Give you your goodnight kiss,
When they tickle you,
As my father no longer can.
Oh, how I pity you,
You children of fools, of cowards, of those who would not take up
The mantle of freedom,
When it was thrust into their grasp,
They dropped it, and instead clutched you.
As my father could not do.

For it was not in his construct to turn his back on the defense of his
loved ones.
Even if it meant he could no longer be there for us.
For me to grow up with his firm hand on my shoulder.
Yet, I feel his hand there now,
As I see you caper uncaring, unknowing, ignorant in your bliss.
I shall not cover my neighbor's living father
For he is thin, as thin as laughing gas that has no meaning and no
lasting power,
Spent in his effect then gone on to raise you in his shallow image.
I feel my father's hand upon my shoulder,
As the tears well unbidden, I stand out on the playground,
My teacher tries to comfort me,
But she is just as repulsive to me as your own father
And for those very reasons.
When her hated hands rest upon my body,
When she sweeps me up to comfort me,
It only deadens the feel of my true father's hands upon my
shoulder.
I cast her off.
I pity you all.
You do not know,
What it is to have a father such as mine.
A father who truly knows the meaning that is blank and blunt in its
absence,
Within the minds of your parents, our teacher,
Their hollow lives and empty minds do not know,
And never shall,
The knowledge of true caring, of sacrifice, for love of me.

Dixon Hill

Kids

"You're just a kid,"

They say sometimes when I open to things.

"Just keep to your own mind, you own self plenty.

We're gonna, um, handle it! No need…"

So I quiet for a time,

But it gnaws at my brain

And my mind knows what's in my heart

And my heart hears my mind and has to speak above the noise

The chatter which claims to know "…just how to go to it."

And I cry, cry out!

They sigh, "What do you know? Um, you're just a kid!"

Like they did when love died.

Did love die?

I don't remember now.

Why?

When did it be?

Show me!

H.E.M.

Our Heroes

Name:
Relation:
Date of Birth:
Age:
Military Branch:
Rank:
Location/Stationed:
Date:

Our Heroes

Name:
Relation:
Date of Birth:
Age:
Military Branch:
Rank:
Location/Stationed:
Date:

The Sandman

The flowers are sleeping
Beneath the moon's soft light
With heads close together
They dream through the night
And leafy trees rock to and fro
And whisper low
Sleep, sleep, lullaby
Oh sleep, my darling child

Now birds that sang sweetly
To greet the morning sun
In little nests are sleeping
Now twilight has begun
The cricket chirps its sleepy song
Its dreamy song
Sleep, sleep lullaby
Oh sleep, my darling child

The sandman comes on tiptoe
And through the window peeps
To see if little children
Are in their beds asleep
And when a little child he finds
Casts sand in his eyes
Sleep, sleep, lullaby
Oh sleep, my darling child

Johannes Brahms (1833-97)

Prayer at Time of Adversity
An Inuit Indian Prayer

I think over again my small adventures.
My fears,
Those small ones that seemed so big,
For all the vital things
I had to get and reach.
And yet there is only one great thing,
The only thing,
To live to see the great day that dawns
And the light that fills the world.

★ ⭐ ★

_____
_____
_____

_____
_____
_____
_____
_____
_____
_____
_____
_____
_____
_____
_____
_____
_____
_____
_____
_____
_____
_____

★ ★ ★

_____

_____

_____

_____

_____

_____

_____

_____

_____

_____

_____

_____

_____

_____

_____

_____

_____

_____

_____

_____

_____

_____

_____

_____

_____

★ ★ ★

Untitled

You wish mommy was still here. It's really hard to get to sleep now. Mommy used to tuck you in and read to you when you were little before she left. You're a big kid now. You're in school with the big kids. Grandma tell you every time she sees you that you're getting to be a big kid. But it's still hard to sleep without mommy sitting next to you, reading to you and rubbing your forehead. Daddy says that mommy will be home after your next birthday, but that's so far away. You miss her so much, you really wish mommy was still here.

You're not even sure where your mommy is. Daddy tried to show you once on a map. He put his finger on a spot and said, "This is where we live." Then he traced his finger all the way across, to the other side of the map, and told you that's where mommy is. You're not sure where that is exactly, just that it's very far away. You asked, "Why can't we go see mommy?" Daddy told you that it's very far away and that you'd need to ride on a boat or airplane to get there. "And it a very dangerous place." He said, "It would be very scary for a little boy." You tried telling him that you were a big kid now, and wouldn't be scared. You don't even need a night light anymore. But he said it would still be scary, he said it would be scary even for him, and your daddy is a big man. You can't imagine anything scaring him.

"If it's such a scary place, why is mommy there? Isn't she scared?" Daddy told you that she's probably a little scared, but she's very brave. "What does brave mean?" You asked. "Brave is when mommy is scared to do something, but she does it anyway because it's very important." That made you feel a little better, knowing that mommy was brave and doing something very important. You went to school and told your teacher what daddy said. She told you that daddy was right. Your mommy was doing very important things. "What's she doing?" You asked. Your teacher told you that she was fighting to make the world safe for democracy. "What's d-e-m-o-c-r-a-c-y?" You asked her. She seemed like she wasn't quite sure. She said that you should ask your daddy. When you asked him, he said that it was what gave people freedom. "What's f-r-e-e-d-o-m?" You asked him. He seemed like he wasn't quite sure. Then he said, "Freedom is hard to explain. It's like when you want to go outside and play. You come and ask me if it's okay and we say it is. Then you go outside and play. That's freedom. Or like when you come home from school and watch cartoons. You can do that because you have freedom. But there are some people who don't have freedom because they don't have democracy. Mommy is fighting to give people freedom." You don't understand this. You always thought fighting was a bad thing to do. And it seems strange that other kids can't go outside and play or watch cartoons. You thought all kids were allowed to do that, unless they were in trouble for doing something bad, like fighting. None of this makes any sense to you. You just know that if mommy were here, she would tuck you in at night and read to you. Then she would kiss you good night and tell you she loves you very much.

You really wish mommy was still here.

Jeremiah Gager

I Am a Piper

If you were to walk along a certain one mile stretch of sandy white beach, on the island of Aruba at sunset, you might see as many as fifty people walking toward the water's edge aimlessly as if sleepwalking. You would see families ascending to their tenth floor balconies of Marriot's, Hyatt's, and Holiday Inns. You would notice teens frozen in place on the sandy volley ball courts as if tranquilized, wild island dogs cease barking as if drugged, happy hour laughter halts, and later afternoon swimmers quickly body surf to shore as if a lifeguard's whistle signaled the sighting of Jaws.

At first, you might think there was a terrible accident on the beach, or maybe a luxury yacht floated too close to shore, you might even speculate that a celebrity like Tom Cruise was spotted walking that white stretch of sand. But at the same time you're imagining this you hear the distinctive sound of bagpipes playing. As the sound gets closer, you watch people place their hands over their hearts, remove hats from their heads, and even wipe tears from their eyes. *Who is playing those bagpipes*, you think, *and why?*

The mystery piper's arms are tan like a weekend golfer's coat of arms, his white legs however indicate he's from a climate where he wears long pants more often than not. His crew cut salt and pepper hair fit his round, wrinkle-free baby face perfectly. His prescription glasses have dark tinted clip-ons to protect his large sparkly blue eyes from the sun. He's barefoot, wearing a faux Tommy Bahamas Hawaiian shirt, khaki shorts, and holding what looks like a bag of groceries in his right crooked arm. The piper is Lieutenant Brian Patrick Shannon, a 52 year old retired Port Authority policeman, a thirty year veteran, 9/11 survivor, and father of four girls. Why does this man play the bagpipes every night for complete strangers in Aruba, when he could be sipping Pina Coladas at his favorite karaoke bar with the rest of the tourists?

Brian Patrick Shannon was born in Bayridge Brooklyn, the middle son of four boys of second generation Irish Catholics. "I started working when at age ten and didn't stop till ten months ago when I retired," says Shannon. "Our family struggled financially back in the 60's and my brothers were in trouble a lot with the law.

It only seemed right that I work and help the family, even at such a young age."

Brian became a New York City cop and was laid off two years later. He then proudly became a Port Authority police officer. Shannon worked at airports, tunnels, bridges, and train stations for the cities of New York and New Jersey. He quickly rose in rank as a Port Authority policeman and his leadership qualities were constantly rewarded. Lieutenant Shannon informs me in a New York accent and his expressive big blue eyes that, "Being a Port Authority cop or any cop is no big deal."

With his hands now talking as if a teacher of sign language, Shannon's voice gets louder as he explains that people think that cops are like characters on Hill Street Blues, NYPD, and those CSI shows. "Hollywood sure does have an imagination. I should write for those programs, you'd be bored to death with the truth, it wouldn't be so glamorous." When asked specifically about his involvement during 9/11, Shannon makes it clear, "Nine-eleven was just another day in the life of a police lieutenant, another day on the job." He tries not to change the expression on his face or the inflection of his voice as he quickly tells me the story with little to no detail and not make much eye contact. "When word got to us at the bus terminal that one of the Twin Towers had collapsed and they needed men, I went down my roster and sent ten men. Nine of them, rookies fresh out of school. They had the most up to date knowledge and knew how to use the brand new Scott air pack equipment, just like the firemen. I directed the rest of my staff on securing the terminal, calming the public, and making ready for further drama and destruction." A very confident Shannon looks me straight in the eyes and says, "My ten men never made it to roll call on nine-twelve." I asked if he had any regrets for sending those men. He said, "No, it's my job and it was their job too. I'm sorry for their families and loved ones, but it's what they sign up for." Besides the passion for being a cop, Lieutenant Shannon developed another passion, the love of playing the bagpipes.

Brian recalls standing along a sidewalk in Brooklyn, on St. Patrick's Day, with some buddies at age twelve. They watched the local school band march by, the neighborhood rotary group sachet in no particular rhythm. Then, like the opening scene of *Braveheart*, came twenty-five handsome, burly men in kilts and knee socks, wearing plaid hats, walking not marching, with a precise beat and Celtic pride written all over their faces. The pipers filled the streets with the sound of *Danny Boy* and as they passed each cluster of onlookers, silence came over each and every person. He saw hats come off, tears run down people's eyes, and hands placed on hearts. The sound from the drones of the piper's instruments magically forced Brian to stand up straight as the hairs on the back of his neck did the same.

He remembers placing his hands, palms in, close to his body like a West Point cadet, ready to salute. He held his head erect while goofy twelve year old thoughts left his head, replaced miraculously with feelings of patriotism, honor, manhood, and ethnic pride. He doesn't remember exactly what part of that outer body experience changed him that day, but at that moment, Brian Patrick Shannon knew he wanted to be a piper.

Officer Shannon played the pipes for thirteen years and then gave it up for ten. During his thirteen years, he played every year in the St. Patrick's Day Parade down Fifth Avenue in New York City. He says he loved playing the bagpipes and always got a kick out of how women want to look up his kilt, especially on St. Patrick's Day when they were leaving an Irish pub. Shannon proceeded to tell me in a very theatrical Cockney Irish accent, "When you're an Irish American, a city cop, and play the pipes, you really know what's right in the world." He felt it was right, but gave up the pipes for ten years to spend more time with his wife and daughters and earn his master's degree. However, on Christmas of 2002, he received a special gift from his family. The card on the box read, "You're The Piper and we miss him." Inside the box was a chanter, the practice instrument for the pipes.

It took a few weeks on the chanter before he took his bagpipes out of the closet and started to play again. He said that, "All the things I hold dear as a policeman, a father, a husband, Irish American, and a human being were profoundly felt when I played the pipes. It was good to get that feeling back again." Shannon realized something even more profound once he started back. He understood why he didn't talk about 9/11. Why he kept his feelings deep inside. He felt that day was a personal attack on his city, his fellow cops, his men, and himself. He chooses not to talk about it.

Shannon attended thirty-three funerals after 9/11. At all thirty-three funerals, fellow police officers played their pipes. Shannon didn't get to do that. "My biggest regret about nine-eleven was that I was not able to bury those men properly by playing Amazing Grace as they entered their final resting place. I did my job as a police lieutenant that day, but I failed to do my job as a piper the days and weeks that followed. I know that will stay with me the same way my brothers will never recover from their role in nine-eleven."

Lieutenant Shannon says he's a happy man. "Why not?" He says, "I'm a retired cop with a great pension, good health, and a wonderful family." Shannon is quick to say however, when summing up his life to date, "I would have to say that first and foremost, I'm a piper. That is what has made me who I am today. Every time I play a song like Amazing Grace, God Bless America, or Danny Boy at a funeral, wedding, birth of a child, or the beaches of Aruba, I do it for every man, woman, and child so that they too can feel what I felt as a twelve year old standing alongside a curb at a St. Patrick's Day Parade in Brooklyn.

"It is probably what all those people feel as they follow me passed hotels, bars, snorkeling boats, and swimming pools down the beach. I am a Piper," says Shannon as he embraces his pipes, gives me a smile and a wink to his daughter Tara and starts to play his next song. He moves along the beach again with that precise walk, leaving his footprints in the sand as he goes. The sun is lowering to the horizon and getting a deeper orange in color, the palm trees whistle their own tune and up ahead you see people looking toward the beach whispering to each other. You see men with hats off, volleyball players kicking sand as if waiting for another team and red faced happy hour regulars holding plastic cups as they walk toward the beach. You can spot the war veterans with hands already over their sand castles before the next wave takes them away. It's sunset and they're all waiting for Lieutenant Brian Patrick Shannon to play his bagpipes…for he is the piper.

A True Story by Cathy Droz

My Dear Charles,

You would be so proud of the children and how they are progressing along. Rupert has been very excited and has learned how to ride a bicycle. Now it's nearly impossible to get him in for his bath and to bed. Our darling daughter has lost her first tooth and was thrilled with her first experience with the tooth fairy. She is saving her tooth for her daddy to see. We are all missing you every day. I want you to know that every evening before retiring we each take a turn kissing your photograph good night. I speak of you each day in order to keep your memory alive in our children's minds. They are so young to have their father away from them for such long periods of time. From the way that they speak of you, I know that you are as vivid and as close to them as the day that you had to leave us. Oh, my dear Charles, how I miss you so. You are a part of my soul. You are my happiness. You are my husband, my life, my love, I can see you when a breeze touches my face and I can feel your caress. I can see you in our children's smiling faces. I can see you in my imagination morning, noon, and night. A loving heart shall never forget. Whenever I hear the thunderstorms of war, I worry so about your safety. I look out of the window at the rain and the lightning and I imagine what you must be going through every day. It takes all of the strength within myself not to allow the tears to flow. I pray to God each day that you will return to the safety of your loving family. I look forward to the blissful day when I shall be blessed by being able to hold you close in my arms. I have been waiting for that special day for so long that when it arrives I may never let go. My heart aches for you at every breathing moment. Please come home, dear Charles, please come home.

Your ever faithful and devoted wife,
Aurora

Dear Lord,

Please bless these children who are the center of your heart. Please give them the strength to understand and work through the pain that they are feeling. Please guide them down the right path and bring people into their lives that will stand by them and love them as much as they deserve. Please forgive them for when they are angry and maybe blame you, even though they may feel completely alone and as if there is no hope, in time they will know you are standing right beside them. Please protect them and help them to grow up strong. To have pride in themselves and the things that they do. To enjoy life and find happiness because happiness is a gift that all your children deserve even if it takes many tears and lots of time to find. Father, God, please let them know, that above all, they are loved. They have always been loved and they will always be loved.

In Jesus' name I pray.

Amen.

X.S.

The Light

The light on the water was a shade of red that called to me. It screamed out over the sand it cast its wet hands upon. I stood staring out over the ocean as the light changed colors in the sky and the loud cannons boomed overhead. It was the fourth of July, fireworks cast lights brightly through the clouds of smoke as the night sky lit up brilliantly. Red fire sparks faded to nothing as the water washed close to my bare feet in the sand.

Remembering, images of red waters, my mind flashed to the fateful day on the beaches of Pearl Harbor in Hawaii. December 7, 1941. The day we entered World War II. That was the day those shores ran red with the blood of innocent soldiers who were killed for being stationed far enough out for Japanese submarines to get their hands on them and get us into a war we tried to avoid.

Infamy they say, that day lives on forever in American hearts. It does. When I look across the ocean this night, I am able to stand here in the dark because of them. On that day, many perished so we could live. In the war, we fought and won, we helped end an evil that waged for years. On this night of celebration, I think back to a time when we were valiant, brave, heroic, standing up for what was right and defending worlds that couldn't defend themselves against tyranny.

Once a brave man said, "Give me liberty or give me death!" That spirit still lives on in the men and women who fight today to end the oppression the world has endured at the hands of madmen. As I still stand in the dark looking up and out over the sea, I smile, knowing how much sacrificing has been done so people like me can live as free as possible even in the modern age among the trials we face.

It's historically in our blood to fight for what's right, to stick up for and help others achieve their own rights and freedoms, for liberty. In this great nation, we celebrate and remember our fallen, for they were and are the brave souls who took it upon themselves to make sure standing by an oceanfront in the middle of the night would be possible to a lone soul who doesn't fight on the shores of a foreign land. With a somewhat heavy heart, we carry with us, the knowledge of such deeds, things done for us, sacrifices made so that we could live.

With every footprint in the sand, a soul watches us from afar, not shouting but quietly watching us. Soothing my soul into further blissful feelings as I stand and watch the sea. My own memories swirl in my head of days gone by, having watched two children grow and thrive in a world made for them by those that fought and continue to fight to keep us safe and free. A smile of thanks graces my face while I continue to stare out and upward into the sky, watching the lights that fill the air signaling freedom, liberty, and justice for all.

Jennifer Oneal Gunn

Our Heroes

Name:
Relation:
Date of Birth:
Age:
Military Branch:
Rank:
Location/Stationed:
Date:

Our Heroes

Name:
Relation:
Date of Birth:
Age:
Military Branch:
Rank:
Location/Stationed:
Date:

★ ★ ★

_____
_____
_____
_____
_____
_____
_____
_____
_____
_____
_____
_____
_____
_____
_____
_____
_____
_____
_____
_____
_____

Taps

Day is gone, gone the sun
From the hills, from the lake
From the sky.
All is well, safely rest
God is nigh.

Thanks and praise, for our days
'Neath the sun, 'neath the stars
'Neath the sky.

Then goodnight, peaceful night
Till the light of dawn shineth bright
God is near, do not fear
Friend, goodnight.

We would like to warmly thank the contributors of this anthology and the readers for purchasing, your proceeds are going to help our soldiers.

www.ingramcontent.com/pod-product-compliance
Lightning Source LLC
LaVergne TN
LVHW051457080426
835509LV00017B/1784